Korean Business Dictionary

Korean
Business
Dictionary

Morry Sofer
General Editor
Peter Yoon
Korean Editor

Schreiber Publishing
Rockville, Maryland

Korean Business Dictionary
Morry Sofer
Peter Yoon

Published by:

Schreiber Publishing
Post Office Box 4193
Rockville, MD 20849 USA
www.schreiberpublishing.com

Library of Congress Cataloging-in-Publication Data

Sofer, Morry.
  Korean business dictionary : English-Korean / Morry Sofer, General Editor ;
Peter Yoon, Korean Editor. -- 1st ed.
      p. cm.
  ISBN 0-88400-320-5 (pbk.)
  1. Business--- Dictionaries. 2. Commerce--Dictionaries. 3. English
language--Dictionaries--Korean. 4. Korean language--Dictionaries--English. I.
Yoon, Peter. II. Title.

HF1002.S565 2006
330.03--dc22

                                                        2006018571

Printed in the United States of America

Introduction

Business language around the world in the twenty-first century is in a state of rapid change. This creates the need for new business dictionaries that are not tied to the past but rather reflect the new global economy. This is particularly true in regard to an English-Korean business dictionary, which brings together two economic systems that are far from identical. The dictionary covers business terms from the United States and their Korean equivalents or, in some cases, Korean definitions.

When it comes to technical terminology in general and the business and computer terms in particular, English is the leader in coining new terms, while Korean is still in the process of creating such terms. The main corollary of this new reality is that even a new English-Korean business dictionary is not going to be exhaustive and definitive. But at least it is a start. It is to be expected that such a dictionary will be updated at least once a year or every two years at the most.

Many of the English business terms in this dictionary are very American-specific. As such, they do not always have equivalent terms in Korean and therefore are explained in some detail.

This dictionary covers many areas of business, such as banking, insurance, real estate, export-import, stock market, and more. In addition, several hundred business-related computer and Internet terms have been included.

Many of the Korean business terms used today are directly copied from English. Some of the English business terms have both a Korean term and a term derived from English. The user of this dictionary is advised not to look upon all the Korean terms herein included as cast in stone. Some may be questioned by business professionals in South Korea. But it goes without saying that the need for this kind of dictionary is urgent and should go a long way in contributing to better trade relations between English-speaking and Korean-speaking business partners.

A

a priori statement
직감적 진술, 추측적 발표
abandonment
포기, 유기
abandonment clause
포기조항
abatement
감소, 경감, 폐지
ABC method
ABC 재고관리 방식
ability to pay
지불능력
abort (*computer*)
중단하다, 중지
above the line
표준 이상의
abrogate
폐기하다
absence rate, absenteeism
결근율, 상습적 결근
absentee owner
부재지주
absolute advantage
절대적인 이점
absolute liability
절대적인 책임
absolute sale
무조건 판매
absorbed
흡수된, 병합된

absorption costing
총체 원가계산
absorption rate
흡수율
abstract of record
등기필증
abstract of title
권리증
abusive tax shelter
세금 도피 수단
accelerated
cost recovery system
(ACRS)
가속 감가상각 방식
accelerated
depreciation
가속 감가상각
acceleration
가속, 조기 상환
acceleration
clause
가속 조항, 조기 상환 조항
accelerator, accelerator
principle
가속도 인자, 가속도 원리
acceptance
승락, 수납, 어음의 인수
acceptance sampling
샘플링 검수
access right
접근 권리

access time
접속 시간
access(*computer*)
액서스, 접속
accession
취득, 상속, 접근
accommodation endorser,
  maker or party
융통어음 배서인
accommodation paper
융통어음
accord and satisfaction
대물변제
account
고객, 거래처, 계좌, 계산서,
계정, 회계, 보고
account executive
고객 회계주임, 증권회사의
고객 거래 중개인
account number
계좌번호, (거래) 구좌번호
account statement
계산서, 거래일람표
accountability
책임, 직책
accountancy
회계업무, 회계학
accountant
회계사, 계리사
accountant 's
  opinion
회계사의 의견
accounting change
회계방침 변경

accounting cycle
회계 주기
accounting equation
회계 등식
accounting error
회계상의 오류
accounting method
회계 방식, 회계 방법
accounting period
회계 기간, 회계 연도
accounting principles,
  accounting standards
회계 원칙, 회계 기준
accounting procedure
회계 절차
accounting rate of return
회계적 이익률
accounting records
회계 기록, 회계 장부
accounting software
회계 소프트웨어
accounting system
회계 시스템
accounts payable
지급 계정, 외상매입 계정
accounts payable ledger
미지불금 원장
accounts receivable
외상매출 계정, 미수금 계정
accounts receivable
  financing
외상 매출 채권 대출
accounts receivable
  ledger
외상 매출금 원장

accredited investor
공인된 투자가
accretion
가치의 증가, 증대, 첨가물,
accrual method
발생주의
accrue
생기다, 발생하다
accrued interest
발생된 이자, 미수 이자,
미불 이자
accrued liabilities
미불 부채, 미불 채무
accrued taxes
미불 세금
accumulated
depletion
누적된 소멸상각
accumulated
depreciation
감가상각 충당금
accumulated
dividend
미불 배당금, 적립 배당금
accumulated earnings
tax or accumulated
profits
유보 수익세, 유보 이익금
acid test
ratio
당좌비율
acknowledgment
승인, 사례
acquisition
취득, 인수

acquisition cost
취득 가격
acre
에이커 (약 1,224 평), 토지
acreage
에이커 수, 면적
across the board
전체에 미치는, 일률적으로
act of bankruptcy
파산(을 위한) 행동
act of god
불가항력
activate (computer)
활성화하다
activate a file
(computer)
파일 활성화
activate a macro
(computer)
매크로 활성화
active cell
(computer)
선택한 셀
active income
능동 소득 (급료, 이자소득)
active market
호황 시장
actual cash value
현금 환산 가치
actual cost
실제 원가
actual damages
실질적 손해
actuarial science
보험 통계학

actuary
보험계리인

ad infinitum
무한히, 영구히

ad item
부가 상품

ad valorem
값에 따라

addendum
추가물, 부록

additional first-year depreciation (tax)
첫해 추가 감가상각

additional mark-on
추가 가격 인상

additional paid-in capital
추가 납입 자본금

add-on interest
추가 금리

adequacy of coverage
보상 범위의 타당성

adhesion contract
부합 계약

adhesion insurance contract
부합 보험 계약

adjective law
부속법, 절차법

adjoining
근접의, 서로 접한, 부근의

adjudication
판결, 선고

adjustable life insurance
조정 가능 생명보험

adjustable margin (computer)
조정 가능 여백

adjustable mortgage loan (AML)
조정 금리 저당 대출

adjustable-rate mortgage (ARM)
변동 금리 저당 대출

adjusted basis or adjusted tax basis
수정 과세 기준

adjusted gross income
조정 후 총소득

adjuster
조정자, 손해 사정인

adjusting entry
조정 기입, 수정 기입

administer
관리하다, 운영하다

administered price
관리 가격

administrative expense
일반 관리비, 경상비

administrative law
행정법

administrative management society
경영관리학회

11

administrative services
  only (ASO)
일반 관리사무에 한정
administrator
관리자, 집행자, 행정가
administrator's
  deed
유산 관리인의 날인증서
advance
선불금, 선불하다, 가불하다
advanced funded
  pension plan
사전 적립식 연금제도
adversary
상대자, 적
adverse opinion
부정적 의견, 반대 의견
adverse possession
불법 점유
advertising
광고, 광고업
advertising
  appropriation
광고비, 광고 충당금
affective behavior
감정적 행동
affidavit
선서서, 진술서, 구술서
affiliated chain
자매 가맹점, 계열 가맹점
affiliated company
계열회사, 자회사
affiliated retailer
가맹 소매업자

affirmative action
차별 철폐조치
affirmative relief
피고자 구제 또는 보상
after market
제 2 차 시장
after-acquired clause
사후 취득 조항
after-acquired property
사후 취득 재산
after-tax basis
세금 공제후 기준
after-tax cash flow
세금 공제후 현금 흐름
after-tax real rate of
  return
세금 공제후 실수익률
against the box
보유 주식의 쇼트세일
age discrimination
연령 차별
agency
대리점, 특약점
agency by
  necessity
필요한 대리점
agent
대리인, 특약점, 알선인
agglomeration
집단, 덩어리
agglomeration
  diseconomies
집단의 비경제성, 집단의
비용증대

aggregate demand
총수요

aggregate income
총소득

aggregate indemnity
(aggregate limit)
총 손해배상 한도액,
총 책임 한도액

aggregate supply
총공급

aging of accounts
receivable or
aging schedule
미수금의 경과 기간 또는
미수금 경과 시간표

agreement
합의(서), 계약(서), 협정(서)

agreement of
sale
매매 계약, 판매 계약

agribusiness
농업 관련 사업, 기업 농업

air bill
항공 화물 운송장

air rights
공중권

airfreight
항공 화물(편)

aleatory contract
사행적 계약

alien corporation
외국 기업

alienation
양도, 이전, 소외

alimony
이혼 수당, 별거 수당

all risk/all peril
전 위험 담보의

allegation
진술, 주장

allocate
할당하다, 분배하다

allocated benefits
분배된 혜택

allocation of resources
자원 분배

allodial
완전 사유지의

allodial system
사유지 제도

allowance
수당, 급여, 용돈, 공제, 할인

allowance for depreciation
감가상각 충당금

allowed time
허용 시간

alternate coding key
(alt key) (computer)
교체키

alternative hypothesis
대립 가설

alternative minimum
tax
최소한의 소득세

alternative mortgage
instrument (AMI)
대체 저당 수단

amass
(재산을) 축적하다, 모으다

amend
수정하다, 개정하다
amended tax return
(세금의) 수정보고
amenities
편의 시설, 문화 시설
american stock exchange
 (AMEX)
아메리칸 증권 거래소
amortization
할부 상환(액)
amortization schedule
할부 상환 계획표
analysis
분석, 해석
analysis of variance
 (ANOVA)
분산 분석법
analysts
분석자들
analytic process
분석 과정
analytical review
분석적 재검토
anchor tenant
주 입주자
animate *(computer)*
동영상화하다, 생명을
불어넣다
annexation
부가물, 첨가, 합병
annual basis
연율 기준으로

annual debt service
연간 지불할 원금과 이자
annual earnings
연간 소득, 연간 수입
annual meeting
연차 주주 총회
annual mortgage constant
연간 저당상수
annual percentage rate
 (APR)
(실질) 연이율
annual renewable term
 insurance
매년 갱신 가능한 정기보험
annual report
연차 보고서, 연보
annual wage
연봉, 연간 임금
annualized rate
연율
annuitant
연금 받는 사람
annuity
연금
annuity due
기말 불입금
annuity factor
연금율, 연금 계수
annuity in advance
선 지급 연금
annuity in arrears
미지불 연금
answer
해결책, 답변, 해답

anticipated holding period
예상 자산 보유 기간
anticipatory breach
기한전 계약 위반
antitrust acts
독점 금지법
antitrust laws
독점 금지법
apparent authority
외견상의 권한
appeal bond
항소 공탁금, 상소 공탁금
appellate court (appeals court)
상소 법원
applet *(computer)*
애플릿
application of funds
자금의 운용
application program *(computer)*
응용 프로그램
application software *(computer)*
응용 소프트웨어
application window *(computer)*
응용 프로그램 창
applied economics
응용경제학
applied overhead
적용된 간접비
applied research
응용 연구

apportionment
배당, 할당, 배분
appraisal
평가, 사정, 감정
appraisal rights
감정권
appraise
감정하다, 평가하다
appraiser
감정사, (세관의) 감정관
appreciate
인정하다, (시세가) 오르다
appreciation
(가격의) 증가, 등귀
appropriate
충당하다, 적당한
appropriated expenditure
할당 지출금
appropriation
지출, 할당, 세출의 승인
approved list
승인 목록
appurtenant
부속의, 종속하는
appurtenant structures
부속건물
arbiter
중재인, 조정자, 결정자
arbitrage
재정거래
arbitrage bond
재정 인수 증권
arbitration
중재, 조절, 중재재판

arbitrator
중재인, 심판자
archive storage
(공)문서 보관소, 기록
보관소
arm's length transaction
이해 당사자간의 거래
array
정렬, 배열, 정렬하다
arrearage
미불금, 연체금액
arrears
지체, 밀림, 연체금
articles of incorporation
회사정관
artificial intelligence
(AI)
인공지능
as is
현상유지, 이대로
asked
요구하는, 청구하는
asking price
제시 가격, 호가
assemblage
조립, 집합
assembly line
일관작업 열, 조립 라인
assembly plant
조립 공장
assess
사정하다, 평가하다
assessed valuation
감정가, 사정 가격

assessment
부과(금), 사정액
assessment of
deficiency
수입 부족액 평가, 결손 평가
assessment ratio
평가액 비율
assessment role
(과세를 위한) 재산 평가서
assessor
(재산) 평가인, (과세)
사정인, (손해) 감정인
asset
자산, 재산
asset depreciation range
(ADR)
자산 감가상각 한도
assign
양도하다, 할당하다
assignee
양수인, 수탁자
assignment
양도, 양도증서
assignment of income
수입 양도(증서)
assignment of lease
임차권의 양도
assignor
양도인
assimilation
동화, 동화작용, 융화
association
협회, 단체, 연합, 조합

assumption of mortgage
저당 인수, (주택)융자금
인수
asterisk *(computer)*
별표, 별표를 하다
asynchronous
비동시성의, 비동기식의
at par
액면 가격으로
at risk
위험한 상태에, 위험을
무릅쓰고
at the close
맨끝에
at the opening
시작에
attachment
첨부서류, 압류, 차압, 구속
attained age
현재의 나이, 현재의 연령
attention
주의, 주목,
attention line
어텐션 라인, 수신인 기입난
attest
증언하다, 증명하다
attorney-at-law
변호사
attorney-in-fact
대리인
attribute sampling
특성 추출(법)
attrition
자연 감소, 소모, 마찰

auction or auction sale
경매
audience
청중, 관객, 청취자
audit
회계감사, 결산
audit program
감사 프로그램
audit trail
감사 추적
auditing standards
회계 기준
auditor
회계감사원
auditor's certificate
감사원의 증명서
auditor's certificate,
  opinion or report
감사원의 증명서, 감사원의
의견서, 감사원의 보고서
authentication
인증, 입증
authorized shares or
  authorized stock
수권 주식
automatic (fiscal)
  stabilizers
자동 (재정) 안전장치
automatic checkoff
자동 노동조합비 공제
automatic
  merchandising
자동 판매기에의한 판매
automatic reinvestment
자동 재투자

automatic withdrawal
자동 인출
auxiliary file
 (computer)
보조 파일
average
평균(치), 보통의
average (daily)
 balance
평균 (일일) 잔고
average cost
평균 비용

average down
분할 매입으로 평균 가격을
낮추다
average fixed cost
평균 고정비용
average tax rate
평균 세율
avoirdupois
상형, 무게
avulsion
(토지의) 자연분리,
분열지

B

baby bond
소액채권
baby boomers
베이비 붐 시대에(1946—
1964) 태어난 사람
back haul
귀로, 역송
back office
(회사의) 배후부문,
비영업부문
back pay
체불 임금
back up (computer)
백업
back up withholding
예비 원청징수
backdating
날짜를 소급시키다
background check
(사람의) 배경조사, 경력
조사
background investigation
(사람의) 배경조사, 경력
조사
backlog
주문잔고, 체화, 비축

backslash (computer)
백슬래시
backspace key
(computer)
백스페이스 키
backup file (computer)
백업 파일
backward vertical
integration
후방 수직적 통합
backward-bending supply
curve
후방굴절 공급곡선
bad debt
불량채권, 회수불능
대출금
bad debt
recovery
불량채권 회수
bad debt reserve
대손 충당금
bad title
불량 권리증서, 가짜
권리증
bail bond
보석금, 보석증서
bailee
수탁자

bailment
위탁, 보석, 보석금
bait and switch
  advertising
과대광고
bait and switch pricing
유인상술 가격설정
balance
차액, 대차계정
balance of payments
지불잔고
balance of trade
무역수지
balance sheet
대차대조표
balance sheet reserve
대차대조표 (퇴직급여)
예비금
balanced mutual fund
균형투자펀드
balloon payment
최종잔액 일괄지불
ballot
투표, 투표용지
bandwidth
(주파수의) 대역폭
bank
은행, 은행에 예금하다
bank holding company
은행 지주회사
bank line
은행 신용한도액

bank trust department
은행 신탁부문
banker's acceptance
은행 인수어음
bankruptcy
파산, 도산
bar
변호사업, 법조
bar code
바코드
bar code label
  (computer)
바코드라벨
bargain and sale
토지매매 계약및
대금지불
bargain hunter
염가품을 찾아다니는
사람
bargaining agent
교섭 대표권자
bargaining unit
교섭 단위
barometer
지표, 변화의 징후
barter
물물교환, 교환하다
base period
기준 시기
base rate pay
기본 급여

base rent
기준 임대료
base-year analysis
기준연도 분석
basic input-output system
(BIOS) *(computer)*
바이오스 (기본 입출력
시스템)
basic limits of liability
기본 책임한도액
basic module *(computer)*
기본 모듈 (독자적 기능을
가진 구성요소)
basic operating system
(computer)
기본 운용 시스템
basis
기초, 기본, 기준, 원칙
basis point
베이시스 포인트 (1/100
퍼센트)
batch application
(computer)
일괄처리 응용 프로그램
batch file *(computer)*
일괄 파일
batch processing
일괄 처리
battery
전지

baud
보드 (데이터 처리 속도
단위)
baud rate *(computer)*
보드 레이트 (데이터 처리
속도)
bear
매도측, 약세측
bear hug
매력적인 가격으로의
기업인수 제의
bear market
약세시장
bear raid
주가 폭락을 노리는
투기꾼의 시도
bearer bond
무기명 채권
before-tax cash flow
세금전 현금흐름
bellwether
선도자, 선행지표
below par
액면가 이하
benchmark
표준가격, 기준점
beneficial interest
(신탁이나 재산의) 수익권
beneficial owner
수익주주, 수익권자

beneficiary
수익자, (보험금의) 수령인
benefit
연금
benefit principle
수익자 부담원칙
benefit-based pension
  plan
수당에 기준한 연금제도
benefits, fringe
부가 혜택, 복리후생 혜택
bequeath
유언으로 증여하다
bequest
유증, 유산
best's rating
베스트 평가사의 평가
beta coefficient
베타 계수
betterment
(부동산의) 개량,
(개량으로 인한 부동산의)
가격인상
biannual
반년 마다의, 1 년에
두번의
bid and asked
매입가와 매도가
bid bond
입찰 보증금
bidding up
값을 올려부름

biennial
2 년에 한 번의, 2 년마다의
big board
뉴욕 증권거래소
big-ticket items
높은 가격의 상품
bilateral contact
쌍무 계약
bilateral mistake
쌍방 과실
bill
계산서, 청구서
bill of exchange
환어음
bill of landing
선하증권
billing cycle
대금청구 주기
binder
가계약
bit error rate *(computer)*
비트 오류율
bit map *(computer)*
비트맵
black list
블랙리스트(요주의 인물
일람표)
black market
암시장
blank cell *(computer)*
빈 셀

blanket contract
일괄계약, 포괄적 계약
blanket insurance
포괄보험
blanket mortgage
포괄적 담보
blanket recommendation
전면적 추천
bleed
적자를 나게하다, 착취
당하다
blended rate
혼합비율
blended value
혼합가격
blighted area
황폐지역
blind pool
위임기업 동맹
blind trust
백지신탁
blister
 packaging
돔 모양의 플라스틱 포장
block
큰 양 (10,000 주 이상의
주식)
block policy
포괄보험증권
block sampling
불록 표본추출

blockbuster
대히트작
blockbusting
블록버스팅 (흑인·소수
민족 등을 전입시켜 백인
거주자에게 불안감을
주어 부동산을 싸게 팔게
하는 수법)
blowout
신규발행 주식의 즉각
완매
blue collar
육체노동자
blue laws
엄격한 법
blue-chip stock
우량주
blueprint
청사진, (상세한) 계획
blue-sky law
창공법, 부정 증권거래
금지법
board of directors
이사회
board of equalization
평등화 위원회
boardroom
(이사회 등의) 회의실
boilerplate
공통 기사, 공통 조항

bona fide
진실한, 성실한
bona fide purchaser
선의의 구매자
bond
채권, 공채증서, 공사채
bond broker
채권 브로커, 채권 중개인
bond discount
채권 할인료
bond premium
채권 할증금
bond rating
채권 신용도
bonded debt
공채(사채)발행 차입금
bonded goods
보세화물
book
(회계)장부
book inventory
장부 목록
book value
장부 가격
book-entry securities
장부 기입 증권
bookkeeper
부기(장부) 계원
bookmark (computer)
북마크
boondoggle
쓸데없는 일

boot
단수결제금, 교환차액
boot (computer)
부트
boot record (computer)
부트 레코드
borrowed reserve
차입 준비금
borrowing power of
securities
증권 매입 능력
bottom
최저가, 바닥
bottom fisher
최저가를 노려서 사는
사람
bottom line
결론, 순손익
Boulewarism
받거나 떠나거나
boycott
보이콧, 불매동맹
bracket creep
세율등급의 점진적 상승
brainstorming
브레인스토밍
branch office
 manager
지점장
brand
상표, 브랜드, 상품

brand association
브랜드의 연관성
brand development
브랜드 개발
brand development index
 (BDI)
브랜드 개발지수
brand extension
브랜드 확장
brand image
브랜드(상표) 이미지
brand loyalty
상표 충성도
brand manager
브랜드(상표) 종합관리자
brand name
상표명
brand potential index
 (BPI)
브랜드 잠재력지수
brand share
상품의 시장점유율
breach
불이행, 위반
breach of contract
계약위반, 계약 불이행
breach of warranty
보증위반, 보증 불이행
breadwinner
집안의 벌이하는 사람,
break
급격한 변화, 중지

break-even
 analysis
손익분기 분석
break-even point
손익분기점
breakup
분산, 붕괴
bridge loan
브리지 론(융자)
brightness (computer)
밝기
broken lot
단주
broker
중개인, 브로커
broker loan rate
증권담보 대출금리
brokerage
중개(업), 중개수수료
brokerage allowance
중개수수료 할인
browser (computer)
브라우저
bucket shop
비밀 증권업자
budget
예산, 예산안
budget mortgage
월 상환금액에 세금과
 보험료가 포함된 모기지
buffer stock
완충재고

building code	**business (adj)**
건축 기준 법규	기업의
building line	**business (n)**
건축 제한선	사업, 업무, 회사
building loan agreement	**business combination**
건축 융자 계약	기업 합동, 합병
building permit	**business conditions**
건축 허가	경기
built-in stabilizer	**business cycle**
자동 안정장치	경기 순환, 사업 주기
bull	**business day**
강세, 상승장	영업일, 평일
bull market	**business ethics**
강세시장, 상승시세	기업 윤리, 사업 윤리
bulletin	**business etiquette**
고시, 게시, 보고	사업 의리, 거래 에티켓
bulletin board system	**business interruption**
(BBS)	사업 중단
전자 게시판 시스템(bbs)	**business reply card**
bunching	상용 반송 엽서
몹시 붐비는, 연달은	**business reply envelope**
bundle-of-rights theory	상용 반송 봉투
부동산 소유주의 종합권리	**business reply mail**
burden of proof	상용 반송 우편물
입증책임	**business risk exclusion**
bureau	사업 위험 배제
국, 안내소, 접수처	**business-to-business**
bureaucrat	**adverting**
관료, 관료적인 사람	기업간의 광고
burnout	**bust-up acquisition**
극도의 피로, 쇠진	해체매수, 파산매수

buy
구입하다, 매수하다
buy down
포인트 지불로 이자율을
낮춤
buy in
되삼, 바이인
buy order
매수주문
buy-and-sell agreeement
상호 판매 협정
buy-back agreement
되사기 약정
buyer
사는 사람, 소비자,
구매자
buyer's market
구매자 시장

buyer behavior
소비자행동
buying on margin
신용구매
buyout
회사(주식)의 매점
buy-sell agreement
매매 계약
buzz words
전문용어
by the book
책대로, 정석대로
bylaws
조례, 부칙, 세칙, 내규,
정관
bypass trust
양도소득세 감소 신탁
by-product
부산물

C

C&F
운임포함

cable transfer
전신환(송금)

cache *(computer)*
캐시

cadastre
토지대장

cafeteria benefit plan
종업원 선택 부가급여

calendar year
역년

call
매수약정

call feature
만기전 상환

call option
콜 옵션, 매수선택권

call premium
상환 프리미엄

call price
매입가격

call report
협의 보고서

callable
만기전 상환 가능한

cancel
해약하다, 취소하다

cancellation clause
해약 조항

cancellation provision clause
해약 규정 조항

capacity
자격, 능력, 용량

capital
자본, 자본금

capital account
자본(금) 계정

capital assets
조정자산, 자본적 자산

capital budget
자본예산

capital consumption allowance
자본소진 허가금액

capital contributed in excess of par value
액면가격 초과분
출자자본

capital expenditure
자본지출

capital formation
자본형성

capital gain (loss)
자본이득(손실)

capital goods
자본재

capital improvement
자본적지출, 설비개량

capital investment
설비 투자, 자본 투자

capital intensive
자본집중적

capital lease
자본 리스

capital loss
자본 손실

capital market
자본 시장

capital nature flight
자본의 자연도피

capital rationing
자본 배분

capital requirement
자본수요, 필요한 자본

capital resource
자본의 원천

capital stock
자본금, 자사주식

capital structure
자본구조, 자본구성

capital surplus
자본 잉여금

capital turnover
자본 회전율

capitalism
자본주의

capitalization rate
자본화율

capitalize
자본화하다, 투자하다

capitalized value
자본화가치

caps
상한, 최고한도

caps lock key *(computer)*
캡스록 키

captive finance
 company
전속 융자회사

cargo
화물, 뱃짐, 적화, 짐

cargo insurance
적하보험, 화물보험

carload rate
화차 전세취급 운임률

carrier
운송업자

carrier's lien
운송업자 담보권

carrot and stick
당근과 채찍의, 회유와
위협의

carryback
(소득세의) 환불액

carrying charge
보관비

carryover
이월, 이월품

cartage
운임, 운반비
cartel
카르텔, 기업연합
case-study method
사례연구 방법
cash
현금
cash acknowledgement
현금 영수증명서
cash basis
현금주의
cash budget
현금 예산
cash buyer
현금 구입자
cash cow
재원, 달러박스,
흑자부문
cash discount
현금 할인
cash disbursement
현금 지출
cash dividend
현금 배당
cash earnings
현금 수입
cash equivalence
현금 등가
cash flow
현금 흐름

cash market
현금 시장
cash on delivery (COD)
현금 인도
cash order
현금 주문
cash payment journal
현금 지급장
cash position
현금 보유량
cash ratio
현금 비율
cash register
금전등록기
cash reserve
현금 준비, 지불 준비
cash surrender value
해약 반려금
cashbook
현금출납장
cashier
현금출납계, 계산원
cashier's check
자기지시수표
casual laborer
자유노동자, 임시노동자
casuality insurance
재해보험, 상해보험
casuality loss
재해손실
catastrophe hazard
대재해 위험

catastrophe policy
대재해 보험증권
cats and dogs
투기적이고 값싼 유가증권
cause of action
소송원인
CD-writer/CD-burner
(computer)
CD에 데이터을 기록하는
장치
cell definition *(computer)*
셀 정의
cell format *(computer)*
셀 포맷
censure
비난, 불신임
central bank
중앙은행
central business district
(CBD)
상업 중심지역
central buying
일괄구입
central planning
집권적 계획, 중앙계획
central processing unit
(CPU) *(computer)*
중앙처리장치
central tendency
중심경향

centralization
중앙집권
certificate of deposit
(CD)
예금증서
certificate of
incorporation
정관, 회사설립증명서
certificate of occupancy
거주증명, 건물
사용허가증
certificate of title
권리증서
certificate of use
사용허가서
certification
증명, 보증
certified check
(은행의) 지불보증수표
certified financial
statement
감사된 재무제표
certified mail
등기우편
chain feeding
연쇄적 공급
chain of command
지휘 계통, 명령 계통
chain store
체인 스토어, 연쇄점

chairman of the board
이사장
chancery
형평법 재판소
change
변경, 교환
change of beneficiary
  provision
수익자 조항의 변경
channel of distribution
유통 경로
channel of sales
판매 경로
character
성격, 특성
character (computer)
문자
charge
청구하다, 청구대금
charge buyer
신용구매자
chart
도표
chart (computer)
도표
chart of accounts
계정과목 일람표
charter
설립면허장, 기본정관,
날인증서
chartist
증권시장 차트분석가

chat forum
  (computer)
채팅 공개토론
chattel
가재, 동산
chattel mortgage
동산양도저당
chattel paper
동산저당증권
check
수표
check digit
검사 숫자
check protector
수표금액 인자기
check register
수표 기입장
check stub
수표떼어주고 남은쪽
check-kiting
공수표 발행,
수표 사기
chief executive officer
최고 경영책임자
chief financial officer
최고 재무책임자
chief operating officer
최고 집행책임자
child and dependent care
  credit
어린이와 부양가족보호
공제

chi-square test
어떠한 가정하의
통계학적 테스트
chose in action
무체동산
churning
과도한 매매권유
CIF
운임보험료 포함
가격조건
cipher
암호, 암호문
circuit
순회, 회로
circuit board *(computer)*
회로기판
civil law
민법
civil liability
시민적 책임의무
civil penalty
민사형벌
claim
손해배상 청구
class
집합, 집단, 클래스
class action b shares
B 주 집단 대표소송
classification
분류
classified stock
선별주, 발행단위 분류주

clause
조항
clean
부채가 없음
clean hands
결백
cleanup fund
최종처리비 기금
clear
(수표) 결제
clear title
저당권 설정이 없는
권리증서
clearance sale
창고정리 판매, 염가판매
clearinghouse
수표교환소
clerical error
기장상 오류
clerk
사무원
client
의뢰인, 고객
clipboard
클립보드
clipboard
 (computer)
클립보드
close
비공개
close corporation plan
주식비공개회사 방식

close out
재고정리품
closed account
폐쇄된 계좌, 차액이 없는
대차계정
closed economy
폐쇄 경제
closed stock
세트 상품
closed-end mortgage
폐쇄식 저당
closed-end mutual fund
폐쇄형 투자신탁
closely held corporation
비공개회사
closing
마감
closing agreement
최종 합의
closing cost
부동산 매매수수료
closing date
마감일, 결산일
closing entry
결산기입
closing inventory
기말재고
closing price or closing
 quote
종가, 종장시세
closing statement
최종 진술, 최종 보고서

cloud on title
권리증서의 저당설정
기록
cluster analysis
집단분석
cluster housing
집단주택
cluster sample
집단 견본추출
cluster sampling
집단 견본추출
code
규칙, 관례
code of ethics
윤리 규범
codicil
추가, 부록
coding of accounts
회계용어의 부호화
coefficient of
 determination
결정계수
coinsurance
공동보험
colatteral assignment
담보의 양도
cold canvass
임의적 고객방문지역
collapsible
 corporation
세금을 납부하지 않고
해산된 기업

collateral
담보물건

collateralize
담보화하다

collateralized mortgage
obligation (CMO)
부동산저당
담보채권

colleague
동업자, 동료

collectible
수집품

collection
수금, 수집,
소장품

collection ratio
대금회수율

collective bargaining
단체교섭

collusion
공모, 결탁

collusive oligopoly
공모과점

column chart/graph
(computer)
열 도표/그래프

combinations
조합, 연합

comfort letter
독립 회계감사원 의견서

command
명령, 지휘

command economy
중앙 통제경제

commencement of
coverage
(보험계약의) 적용시작

commercial
상용의, 상업의

commercial bank
상업은행

commercial blanket
bond
상업 포괄채권

commercial broker
상업 중개인

commercial credit
insurance
상업 보증보험

commercial forgery
policy
상업 위조보험

commercial forms
상업서식

commercial health
insurance
상업 건강보험

commercial law
상법

commercial loan
은행 융자, 상업 융자

commercial paper
기업어음, 유가증권

commercial property
영업용 부동산

commercial property
  policy
영업용 부동산 보험
commingling of
  funds
기금의 합동운용
commission
수수료, 위원회
commission broker
중개인
commitment
판매계약, 약속, 의무
commitment free
계약 수수료
commodities
  futures
선물상품, 상품 선물거래
commodity
상품, 물품
commodity cartel
상품 카르텔
common area
공용 구역, 공통 구역
common carrier
공공운송회사, 전화회사
common disaster clause or
  survivorship clause
일반 재해조항 또는
생존자 취득권 조항
common elements
공통요소
common law
관습법, 불문률, 민법

common stock
보통주식, 자본금
common stock equivalent
보통주식 상당증권
common stock fund
보통주식 기금
common stock ratio
보통주식률
communications
  network
통신망
communism
공산주의
community association
지역자치회
community property
공유재산제
commutation right
지불방법을 변경할 권리
commuter
통근자
commuter tax
통근세
co-mortgagor
공동저당권 설정자
company
기업, 회사, 친구
company benefits
회사의 혜택
company car
회사 (업무용) 자동차
company union
어용조합, 기업별조합

comparable worth
남녀 동등 임금원칙

comparables
비교 부동산

comparison shopping
경쟁품조사

comparitive finacial
  statements
비교 재무제표

comparitive negligence
비교 과실, 과실 상쇄

compensating balance
양건예금, 보상예금

compensating error
보상오차

compensation
수당, 보상

compensatory stock
  options
보상적 자사주 구입권

compensatory time
보상적으로 일을 쉰시간

competent party
법적 계약 자격자

competition
경쟁

competitive bid
경쟁 입찰

competitive party
경쟁 당사자

competitive party
  method
경쟁 당사자 방법

competitive strategy
경쟁 전략

competitor
경쟁 기업

compilation
편집, 편찬

compiler
편집자

complete audit
정밀 감사, 완전 감사

completed contract
  method
공사완성 기준

completed operations
  insurance
공사완성보험

completion bond
완성보증채권

complex trust
복합 신탁

compliance audit
준거감사, 준수감사

compliant
(법령을) 준수하는

component part
구성요소

composite depreciation
복합상각

composition
일부변제금, 타협, 화해

compound growth
  rate
복합 성장률

compound interest
복리 이자
compound journal
 entry
복식 부기
comprehensive annual
 finacial report (CAFR)
총괄 연간 재무제표
comprehensive insurance
총괄보험
compress (computer)
압축하다
comptroller
재무부장, 감사관
compulsory arbitration
강제 중제
compulsory insurance
강제 보험
compulsory retirement
강제 퇴직
computer
전자계산기, 컴퓨터
computer-aided
 (computer)
컴퓨터 지원에 의한
concealment
은폐, 은익
concentration banking
집중적 예금
concept test
구상실험, 개념실험
concern
이해관계, 염려

concession
특권부여, 양보
conciliation
조정
conciliator
조정자
condemnation
(재산등의) 수용, 접수,
유죄판결
condition precedent
정지조항, 선행조건
condition subsequent
해제조항, 후행조건
conditional contract
조건부 계약
conditional sale
조건부 매매
conditional-use
 permit
조건부 사용허가
conference call
통화회의
confidence game
신용사기
confidence interval
신뢰 구간
confidence level
신뢰성 수준
confidential
비밀의, 기밀의
confirmation
확인, 조회

conflict of interest
이해상충
conformed copy
합법적 복사
confusion
혼란, 혼동
conglomerate
복합 기업
conservatism,
 conservative
보수주의, 보수적인
consideration
고려 사항
consignee
수탁자, 하수인
consignment insurance
위탁품 보험
consignor
위탁자, 송하인
consingment
위탁, 위탁판매
consistency
일관성
console
콘솔
consolidated financial
 statement
연결 재무제표
consolidated tax
 return
연결 납세 신고서
consolidation loan
연결 융자

consolidator
통합정리자
consortium
조합, 공동사업체
constant
정관, 일정의
constant dollars
불변 가격
constant-payment loan
일정 지불융자
constituent company
구성회사
constraining (limiting)
 factor
제약 요소
construction loan
건설 융자
constructive notice
의제 통지, 추정적 통지
constructive receipt of
 income
추정 소득수령
consultant
상담역, 고문
consumer
소비자
consumer behavior
소비자 행동
consumer goods
소비재, 소비자 상품
consumer price index
 (CPI)
소비자 물가지수

consumer protection
소비자 보호
consumer research
소비자 조사
consumerism
소비자운동,
소비자(우선)주의
consumption function
소비 함수
container ship
컨테이너선
contestable clause
문제 조항, 이의 조항
contingencey fund
우발 손실 준비금
contingency planning
비상사태 계획
contingency table
분할표
contingent fee
성공 보수
contingent liability
우발채무, 불확정책임
contingent liability
 (vicarious liability)
우발채무(대리채무)
continuing education
계속적인 교육
continuity
계속성
continuous audit
계속적 감사

continuous process
연속 공정
continuous production
연속 생산
contra-asset account
자산 차감계정
contract
계약
contract carrier
계약 운송업자
contract of indemnity
손해담보계약
contract price
 (tax)
계약가격(세)
contract rate
계약 요금
contract rent
계약 임차료
contraction
축소, 단축
contractor
청부인, 청부회사
contrarian
역투자가
contrast
 (computer)
명암대비
contribution
기부금, 보험료
contribution profit,
 margin
공헌 이익

contributory negligence
기여 과실
contributory pension plan
갹출 연금제
control
관리, 지배
control account
통제계정,
포괄계정
control key (ctrl)
  (computer)
컨트롤 키
controllable costs
통제 가능 원가
controlled company
자회사,
피지배회사
controlled economy
통제경제
controller
회계검사관
controlling interest
경영지배권
convenience sampling
간이표본 방법
conventional mortgage
무보증 저당대부,
전통적인 저당대부
conversion
환산
conversion cost
가공비

conversion factor for
  employee contributions
종업원기여 환산계수
conversion parity
전환 동량
conversion price
전환 가격
conversion ratio
전환 비율
convertible term life
  insurance
전환가능 정기생명보험
convertibles
태환증권
convey
양도하다,
운반하다
conveyance
양도, 운반
cooling-off period
냉각기간
co-op
공동주택
cooperative
공동의, 협동조합
cooperative advertising
공동광고, 협동광고
cooperative apartment
공동주택 아파트
copy-protected (computer)
복사방지
copyright
저작권

cornering the
  market
시장독점
corporate bond
사채
corporate campaign
기업의 캠페인
corporate equivalent
  yield
회사채 세금후 동등이율
corporate strategic
  planning
기업 전략 계획
corporate structure
기업 구조
corporate veil
기업 연막
corporation
기업, 주식회사,
법인
corporeal
유형의,
물직적인
corpus
원금, 자본금
correction
수정, 보정
correlation coefficient
상관 계수
correspondent
통신원, 거래처
corrupted
부패한

corrupted *(computer)*
오류가 있는, 망가진
cosign
공동서명자
cost
원가, 비용
cost accounting
원가 계산, 원가 회계
cost application
원가 배분
cost approach
원가법
cost basis
원가기준,
원가주의
cost center
원가 중심점
cost containment
비용 억제
cost method
원가법, 원가주의
cost objective
비용 목표
cost of capital
자본 비용
cost of carry
보유 비용
cost of goods
  manufactured
제조 원가
cost of goods
  sold
판매 원가

cost overrun
비용초과
cost records
원가 기록
cost-benefit analysis
비용편익 분석
cost-effectiveness
비용효과
cost-of-living adjustment
(COLA)
생계비 조절
cost-push inflation
비용압력 인플레이션
co-tenancy
부동산 공동세입,
공동보유
cost-plus contract
원가가산계약
cottage industry
가내공업
counsel
법률고문, 고문변호사
counterclaim
반대요구
countercyical policy
경기대책
counterfeit
위조, 모조품
countermand
취소 명령, 반대 명령
counterroffer
역청약, 수정청약

coupon bond
이자부 사채
court of record
기록재판소
covariance
공분산
covenant
계약조항, 날인증서
covenant not to
compete
비경쟁약속
cover
보상범위, 보상(하다)
covered option
커버드 옵션
cracker
불법침입하여 해를 끼치는
자
craft union
직종별조합
crash
실패, 파산, 붕괴
crash (computer)
(시스템의) 고장
credit requirements
자금수요, 신용 필요조건
creative black book
창자적 일에 종사하는
사람이나 회사의
디렉토리
creative financing
이반 모기지이외의 융자

credit
신용, 채권
credit analyst
신용분석가
credit balance
차변 잔액,
여신 잔액
credit bureau
신용조사기관
credit card
신용카드
credit order
신용 주문
credit rating
신용 등급
credit risk
신용 위험
credit union
신용조합
creditor
채권자
creeping inflation
잠행성 인플레이션
critical path method
(CPM)
크리티컬 패스 분석법
critical region
위험역, 기각역
crop (computer)
잘라내다
cross
교차, 교차하다

cross merchandising
상호 판매
cross purchase
 plan
상호 구매 계획
cross tabulation
교차 도표작성
cross-footing
금액의 교차검증
crowd
거래소 회원 그룹
crowding out
이자율을 높이기 위한
정부의 지출증가
crown jewels
중요부문
crown loan
이자 세금을 줄이기 위한
가족사이의 대부
cum dividend, cum rights
 or cum warrant
배당부, 권리부 또는
보증부
cumulative dividend
누적 배당
cumulative liability
중복 책임
cumulative preferred
stock
누적적 우선주
cumulative voting
누적 투표, 집중 투표

curable depreciation	curtesy
회복 가능 가치하락	홀아비 유산권
currency futures	curtilage
통화 선물	주택에 딸린 땅
currency in circulation	custodial account
유통 통화	보관구좌
current	custodian
유통, 유동	관리인, 보관인
current asset	custody
유동자산	보관, 관리, 보호
current assumption whole life insurance	custom profile
현행인수의 종신보험	고객정보
current cost	customer
현행 원가, 현재 원가	고객, 거래처
current dollars	customer service
현 시가	고객 서비스
current liabilities	customer service representative
유동 부채	고객 서비스 담당자
current market value	customs
현행 시장 가격	세관
current ratio	customs court
유동 비율	관세재판소
current value accounting	cutoff point
현행 가치 회계, 시가 회계	결산일, 마감일
current yield	cyberspace (computer)
현재 수익	사이버 스페이스
cursor (computer)	cycle billing
커서	주기적 청구서 작성
curtailment in pension plan	cyclic variation
연금제도의 축소	순환 변동
	cyclical demand
	순환적 수요

cyclical industry
순환 산업

cyclical stock
순환주

cyclical unemployment
주기적실업

D

daily trading limit
일일 거래한도
daisy chain
연쇄
damages
손해(배상금)
data
데이터, 자료
data collection
   (computer)
데이터 수집
data maintenance
   (computer)
데이터 보수, 데이터유지
data processing insurance
데이터 처리 보험
data retrieval (computer)
데이터 검색
data transmission
   (computer)
데이터 전송
database
데이터베이스
database management
데이터베이스 관리
date of issue
발행일
date of record
기록일, 권리확정일

dating
일부기입
de facto corporation
사실상의 회사
dead stock
사장품, 불량재고
dead time
부동 시간
deadbeat
빚을 떼어먹는 사람
dead-end job
장래성이 없는 직업
deadhead
무능한 사람
deadline
최종기한
dealer
판매업자
death benefit
사망 혜택금
debasement
가치저하, 품질저하
debenture
무담보사채
debit
차변
debit memorandum
차변전표

debt
부채, 채무
debt coverage
  ratio
부채회수비율
debt instrument
채권
debt retirement
채권 환수
debt security
채무 증권
debt service
부채 상환
debtor
채무자
debt-to-equity ratio
부채 비율
debug
  (computer)
(프로그램의) 잘못을
고치다
decentralization
분산(화), 분권(화)
deceptive advertising
허위 광고,
확대 광고
deceptive packaging
허위 포장
decision model
결정 모델
decision package
몇개의 결정사항

decision support system
  (DSS)
의사결정 지원 시스템
decision tree
의사결정 분지도
declaration
선언
declaration of estimated
  tax
견적세 신고
declaration of trust
신탁 선언
declare
선언하다
declining-balance
  method
체감잔액법
decryption
  (computer)
암호 해독
dedicated line
전용회선
dedication
전용, 헌신
deductibility of employee
  contributions
종업원 부담금의 공제성
deduction
공제, 공제액
deductive reasoning
연역법
deed
날인증서, 양도증서

deed in lieu of foreclosure
재산을 유질처분전에
대출자에게 돌려주는
행위
deed of trust
신탁증서
deed restriction
토지사용권을 제한하는
양도증서
deep discount bond
초활인채권
defalcation
부당 유용
default
채무 불이행
default *(computer)*
디폴트 값
default judgment
결석재판,
결석판결
defeasance
무효, 권리소멸
defective
불량품
defective title
거래할 수 없는 소유권
defendant
피고인
defense of suit against
insured
피보험자에 대한 소송

변호
defensive securities
가격안정성 증권
deferred account
이연 계정
deferred billing
이연 청구
deferred charge
이연 비용
deferred compensation
이연 보상
deferred compensation
plan
보수이연 계획
deferred contribution
plan
이연분담금제도
deferred credit
이연대변 항목
deferred group
annuity
거치 그룹 연금
deferred interest bond
이연된 이자 채권
deferred maintenance
이연된 보수유지비
deferred payments
지불의 연기, 후불
deferred profit-sharing
거치형 이익분배
deferred retirement
연기된 은퇴

deferred retirement credit	degression
연기된 은퇴 크레딧	감소
deferred wage increase	deindustrialization
연기된 급료인상	산업의 공동화, 역공업화
deferred-payment annuity	delegate
지불 연기된 연금	대표
deficiency	delete *(computer)*
부족(액)	딜리트, 삭제
deficiency judgment	delete key (del *(computer)*)
부족분 지급 판결	딜리트 키
deficiency letter	delinquency
정정 지시서	체납, 의무 불이행
deficit	delinquent
결손금,	의무 불이행의,
손실금	직무태만의
deficit financing	delisting
적자재정	상장 폐지
deficit net worth	delivery
결손 순자산	인도, 배송
deficit spending	delivery date
적자지출, 초과지출	납기일, 인도일
defined contributuion pension plan	demand
확정된 기여연금제도	요구, 수요
defined-benefit pension plan	demand curve
연금액 보증제도	수요곡선
deflation	demand deposit
디플레이션, 통화수축	요구불예금
deflator	demand loan
가격수정인자	단기 융자,
defunct company	당자 대월
죽은 회사	demand note
	요구불수표

demand price
수요 가격, 가치
demand schedule
수요 예정표
demand-pull inflation
수요에의한 인플레이션
demarketing
역 마케팅, 수요억제
선전활동
demised premises
양도건물(토지)
demographics
인구통계
demolition
파괴, 해체
demonetization
통용금지, 폐화
demoralize
사기를 꺾다
demurrage
체선료, (차량의)
유치료
demurrer
이의(신청자), 항변(자)
denomination
액면금액, (화폐의) 단위
density
밀도
density zoning
밀도 구분
department
부, 부문

dependent
부양가족
dependent coverage
부양가족 보상
depletion
소모, 고갈, 감모상각
deposit
예금, 보증금
deposit administration
 plan
예금관리제도
deposit in transit
미달예금, 은행 미기입
예금
deposition
조서, 증언증서
depositors forgery
 insurance
예금자문서 위조보험
depository trust company
 (DTC)
투자신탁회사
depreciable life
감가상각 기간
depreciable real
 estate
감가상각 부동산
depreciate
가격이 저하하다
depreciated cost
감가상각 원가
depreciation
감가상각

depreciation recapture
감가상각액 재징수
depreciation reserve
감가상각 적립금
depression
불황, 불경기
depth interview
심층 면접
deregulation
규제 완화, 규제 철폐
derived demand
간접 수요
descent
하강, 상속
description
설명서, 기술
descriptive memorandum
설명적 비망록
desk
편집부, 책상
desktop publishing
탁상출판
despriptive statistics
기술통계학
destination file (network)
(computer)
목적파일
detail person
꼼꼼한 사람
devaluation
평가 절하
developer
개발업자

development
개발, 발전
development stage
enterprise
개발단계 기업
developmental drilling
 program
경제성이 증명된 유정에
굴착함
deviation policy
이탈행위에 대한 방침
devise
(부동산의) 유증
disability benefit
장애 혜택
diagonal expansion
대각선적 확장
dialup
다이얼 호출식
diary
일기, 일지
differential
advantage
특이한 이점
differential analysis
미분 분석
differentiation
strategy
차별화전략
digits deleted
삭제된 숫자
dilution
희석(화)

diminishing-balance
 method
체감잔액법
diplomacy
외교
direct access
직접 접근
direct charge-off
 method
손실 직접처리 방식
direct cost
직접원가, 직접비
direct costing
직접원가계산
direct financing lease
직접금융 리스
direct investment
직접 투자
direct labor
직접 작업
direct liability
직접 채무
direct marketing
직접 마케팅
direct material
직접 재료
direct overhead
직접 간접비
direct production
직접 생산
direct response
 advertising
직접 반응 광고

direct sales
직접 판매
direct-action advertising
직접 해동 광고
directed verdict
지시 판결
director
이사, 중역
directorate
이사회, 관리직
direct-reduction mortgage
원금의 일부와 이자를 매
상환에 같이해야하는
모기지
disability buy-out
 insurance
장애매수보험
disability income
 insurance
장애 소득 보상보험
disaffirm
부인하다, 파기하다
disbursement
지출, 지급
discharge
해제, 해고, 면책
discharge in bankruptcy
파산 면책
discharge of lien
담보권 취소
disclaimer
거부, 부인

disclosure
공시, 공개
discontinuance of
 plan
계획 중단
discontinued operation
중단된 영업 활동
discount
할인
discount bond
할인 채권
discount broker
어음할인 중개인
discount points
할인 포인트
discount rate
할인율
discount window
할인 창구
discount yield
할인 수익률
discounted cash flow
현금흐름할인
discounting the news
뉴스를 기대하고 스탁을
거래함
discovery
발견
discovery sampling
색출표본조사
discrepancy
불일치

discretion
재량권, 자유재량
discretionary cost
자유재량원가
discretionary
 income
자유재량소득
discretionary policy
자유재량정책
discretionary spending
 power
자유재량 소비능력
discrimination
차별(대우)
diseconomies
비용 증대
dishonor
불명예
disinflation
디스인플레이션
disintermediation
비중개
disciplinary layoff
규정위반에 의한 직원의
해고
disjoint events
동시에 일어날 수없는
사건들
disk (computer)
디스크
disk drive (computer)
디스크 드라이브

dismissal
해고
dispatcher
급파하는 사람
disposable income
가처분 소득
dispossess
소유권 박탈
dispossess proceedings
소유권 박탈 행위
dissolution
해산, 해제
distressed property
차압 부동산 물건
distribution
유통, 분배
distribution
  allowance
유통 호용금
distribution cost
  analysis
유통 경비 분석
distributor
판매업자, 소매업자
diversification
분산 투자, 다각 경영
diversified company
다각경영 기업
divestiture
기업분할, 자산의 분할
dividend
배당, 이익배당금, 공채
이자액

dividend addition
추가 배당
dividend exclusion
공제 배당
dividend payout ratio
배당 지급률
dividend reinvestment
  plan
배당 재투자 제도
dividend requirement
배당 필요액
dividend rollover plan
배당일에 스탁을
소유하여 배당금을
모의는 계획
dividends payable
미지급 배당금
division of labor
분업
docking
결합
docking station
  (computer)
도킹 스테이션
documentary evidence
문서적 증거
documentation
문서, 서류
doing business as (DBA)
비지니스에 사용하는 이름
dollar cost averaging
스탁이나 뮤추얼 펀드를
매월 일정한 금액 매입함

dollar drain
달러 유출
dollar unit sampling
  (DUS)
달러단위 견본추출
dollar value lifo
달러 금액기준 재고조사
domain name system
도메인 이름 시스템
domestic corporation
내국 법인
domicile
주소
dominant tenement
분할된 일부 토지
donated stock
증여 주식
donated surplus
증여 잉여금
donor
기증자
double (treble) damages
2 배(3 배)의 피해
double click
  (computer)
더블 클릭
double declining
  balance
이중체감잔액
double precision
2 배 정밀도
double taxation
이중과세

double time
임금의 2 배 지불시간
double-digit inflation
두자리 수의 인플레이션
double-dipping
연금외 급료
double-entry
  accounting
복식부기
dow theory
다우이론
dower
과부유산권
down tick
기업활동의 악화
download (computer)
다운로드
downpayment
자기투자자본, 할부의 첫
지불금
downscale
규모를 축소하다
downside risk
가능 손실액
downstream
하류에서
downtime
중단 시간
downturn
경기의 하강
downzoning
다운존화하다

dowry
결혼지참금

draft
환어음, 도면

draining reserves
준비금 고갈, 준비금 유출

draw
인출

draw tool *(computer)*
드로 도구

drawee
어음 수취인

drawer
어음 발행인

drawing account
인출계정

drive *(computer)*
드라이브

drop-down menu (pull-down menu) *(computer)*
드롭다운 메뉴(풀다운
메뉴)

drop-shipping
생산자 직송

dry goods
직물, 포목

dual contract
이중계약

due bill
차용증서

due-on-sale clause
부동산을 매각하면
채무의 상환기일이
만기가 되는 조건

dummy
인체 모형

dumping
투매

dun
빚 독촉장

duplex copying (printing)
(computer)
양면 인쇄

duplication of
benefits
중복 수당

duress
강요, 강박

dutch action
값을 깎아 내려가는 경매

duty
의무, 관세

E

each way
수수료 각자 부담
early retirement
조기 퇴직
early retirement benefits
조기 퇴직 수당
early withdrawal penalty
만기전 인출 벌칙금
earned income
노동 소득
earnest money
보증금
earnings and profits
소득과 이익
earnings before
taxes
세금 공제전 소득
earnings per share
1 주당 이익
earnings report
소득 보고서
easement
지역권
easy money
저금리 돈
econometrics
계량경제학
economic
경제의, 경제학상의

economic analysis
경제 분석
economic base
경제 기반
economic
depreciation
경제적 감가
economic freedom
경제적 자유
economic growth
경제 성장
economic growth
rate
경제 성장율
economic indicators
경제 지표
economic life
경제적 내용연수, 경제적
수명
economic loss
경제적 손실
economic rent
경제 지대
economic sanctions
경제적 제재
economic system
경제 제도
economic value
경제 가치

economics
경제학
economies of scale
규모의 경제
economist
경제학자, 경제전문가
economy
경제, 경제성, 경제계
edit *(computer)*
편집, 편집하다
effective date
효력 발생일, 발효일
effective debt
유효 부채
effective net worth
유효 순자산
effective rate
실효율
effective tax rate
유효세율
efficiency
능률, 효율성
efficient market
효율적 시장
efficient portfolio
효율적 포트폴리오
eject
쫓아내다, 퇴거시키다
eject *(computer)*
이젝트
ejectment
부동산 점유 회복 소송

elasticity of supply and
  demand
수요와 공급의 탄력성
elect
선거하다, 선출하다
electronic mail
  (email)
전자우편(이메일)
emancipation
(노예등의) 해방
embargo
수출 금지, 통상 금지
embed
끼워넣다, 깊이 간직하다
embed *(computer)*
임베드
embezzlement
횡령, 착복
emblement
근로 과실, 작물취득권
eminent domain
사용권
employee
종업원
employee association
종업원 조합 (협회)
employee benefits
종업원 복리후생비 (혜택)
employee contributions
종업원 부담금
employee profit
  sharing
종업원 이익공유제도

employee stock option
종업원 자사 구입제도

employee stock ownership
plan (ESOP)
종업원 지주제도, 우리
사주제도

employer
사용자, 고용주

employer interference
고용자 개입

employment agency
직업소개소

employment contract
고용계약

enable (computer)
작동시키다

enabling clause
권한 부여조항

encoding
부호화

encroach
침입하다, 잠식하다

encroachment
불법침입, 침락

encryption
암호화

encumbrance
채무, 저당, 유치권

end of month
월말

end user (computer)
최종 사용자

endorsement or
indorsement
배서, 이서

endowment
기부, 기부금, 기금,
양로자금

energy tax credit
에너지 세금 공제
(크레딧)

enjoin
명령하다,
금지하다

enterprise
사업, 기업,
조직체

enterprise zone
기업 지구

entity
기업 실체, 법적 실체,
지분

entrepreneur
기업가

entry-level job
초보적인 일

environmental impact
statement (EIS)
환경영향 보고서

EOM dating
월별 말일 기입

equal opportunity
employer
기회균등주의 고용주

equal protection of the
  laws
법률의 균등보호

equalization board
사정 평준국

equilibrium
균형, 평형

equilibrium price
균형 가격

equilibrium quantity
균형 수량

equipment
장치, 설비, 기기

equipment leasing
설비 리스,

장비 리스

equipment trust bond
설비신탁채권

equitable
공평한, 공정한,

형평법상의

equitable distribution
공정한 분배

equity
지분, 자기자본

equity financing
자기자본조달, 주식

발행에 의한 자본조달

equity method
지분법

equity of redemption
상환권, 회수의 권리

equity REIT
부동산 투자신탁

equivalent taxable yield
과세 대상 동등 이율 산출

erase *(computer)*
지우다, 삭제, 소거

error
오류

error message
  (computer)
오류 메세지

escalator clause
신축 조항

escape key (esc)
  (computer)
이스케이프 키

escheat
복귀재산, 몰수재산

escrow
조건부 증서, 조건부

날인증서

escrow agent
조건부 날인증서 수탁자

espionage
스파이 활동, 첩보 활동

essential industry
기간산업

estate
부동산 권리, 개인재산,

유산

estate in reversion
복귀 부동산권

estate in severalty
단독 보유 재산권
estate planning
자산 계획
estate tax
상속세
estimate
견적, 추정, 평가,
견적서
estimated tax
예정 납세액
(세금)
estimator
평가자, 견적인
estoppel
금반어
estoppel certificate
금반어 증서
estovers
필요물, 별거 수당
ethical, ethics
도덕, 윤리, 윤리상의
euro
유로
European Common
  Market
유럽 공동 시장
European Economic
  Community (EOC)
유럽 경제 공동체
eviction
추방, 축출

eviction, actual
현실적 추방
eviction,
  constructive
건성적 추방
eviction, partial
부분 추방
evidence of title
권리서
exact interest
완전 이자, 정확한 금리
« except for » opinion
감사인의 감사불가의견
excess profits tax
초과 이윤세
excess reserves
과잉 준비금
exchange
교환, 환어음, 거래소
exchange control
어음관리, 외국환 관리
exchange rate
환율, 환산률
excise tax
물품세, 국내소비세
exclusion
비과세, 공제
exclusions
제외, 면책,
공제금액
exculpatory
면책

ex-dividend rate
배당락 비율
execute
실행하다, 집행하다
executed
이행 완료
executed contract
이행 완료 계약
execution
실행, 집행, 강제집행
executive
임직원, 중역, 행정부
executive committee
집행위원회
executive perquisites
중역의 특별대우
executor
유언집행자, 상속재산
관리인
executory
미이행, 행정상의
exempt securities
면제 증권
exemption
면제, 면세
exercise
행사(하다)
exit interview
퇴직자 면접
ex-legal
불법의,
비합법적인

expandable
확장가능한
expandable *(computer)*
확장성
expansion
확대, 발전
expected value
기대치, 기대 가치
expense
비용, 원가,
경비
expense account
경비 계정
expense budget
비용 예산
expense ratio
경비 비율
expense report
경비 보고서
experience rating
경험 비율법
experience refund
경험 비율법에의한
환급금
expert power
전문가의 힘
expiration
만기, 소멸
expiration notice
만기일 통보
exploitation
불법 이용, 착취

exponential smoothing
지수평활법
export
수출(하다)
Export-Import Bank (EXIMBANK)
수출입은행
exposure
탄로, 폭로
exposure draft
공개 초안
express
명시적 보증, 명백한 보증, 급행
express authority
명시적 권한
express contract
명시적 계약
extended coverage
확장 담보
extended coverage endorsement
확장 담보 승인, 확장 담보 배서
extension
연장, 채부 변재

extension of time for filing
제출 기한 연장
extenuating circumstances
경감 사유, 정상을 참작해서
external audit
외부 감가
external documents
외부 자료
external funds
외부 자금
external report
외부의 보고서
extra dividend
특별 배당
extractive industry
채취 산업
extraordinary dividends
임시 배당
extraordinary item
임시 항목
extrapolation
추론, 외삽법

F

f statistic
f 통계
fabricator
조립제조업자, 가공업자
face amount
액면 금액
face interest value
액면 금리
face value
액면가, 표시가
facility
시설, 설비, 편익
facsimile
팩스
factor analysis
요인 분석
factorial
계승
factoring
팩토링, 매출채권의 매각
factory overhead
제조간접비
fail to deliver
인도 불이행
fail to receive
인수 불이행
failure analysis
실패분석

fair market rent
공정 시장 임대료
fair market value
공정 시장 가치
fair rate of return
공정 수익율
fair trade
공정 거래
fallback option
예비 선택권
fallen building clause
파괴 건물 계약
false advertising
허위 광고, 불량 광고
family income policy
가족 소득 보험
family life cycle
가족 생활 주기
family of funds
자금군
FAQ (frequently asked questions)
자주 묻는 질문
farm surplus
잉여농산물
fascism
파시즘, 독재적 국가
사회주의

fast tracking
빠른 승진
fatal error
치명적 오류
fatal error
(computer)
치명적 오류
favorable trade balance
무역 수지의 흑자
feasibility study
실행 가능성 조사
featherbedding
생산 제한 행위
fed wire
연방 준비 은행간 통신망
federal deficit
재정 적자
Federal Deposit
  Insurance Corporation
  (FDIC)
연방 예금 보험회사
federal funds
연방 준비 은행 준비금
federal funds rate
준비금 이율
Federal Reserve Bank
연방 준비 은행
Federal Reserve Board
  (FRB)
연방 준비 제도 이사회
Federal Reserve System
  (FED)
연방 준비 제도

Federal Savings and Loan
  Association
연방 저축 대부조합
fee
요금, 수수료
fee simple or fee simple
  absolute
단순 부동산권
feeder lines
지선
FHA mortgage loan
연방주택국 주택융자금
fidelity bond
신용(책임)보험,
신원보증
fiduciary
수탁자
fiduciary bond
수탁자 보증서
field staff
현장직원
field theory of
  motivation
인간 동기부여 현장 이론
file
파일
file backup (computer)
파일 백업
file extension (computer)
파일 확장
file format (computer)
파일 포맷

file transfer protocol
 (FTP)
파일 전송 프로토콜

fill or kill (FOK)
즉시 실행 주문

filtering down
좋은 동네에서
고소득자들이 떠나고
저소득자만 남음

final assembly
최종 조립

finance charge
재무 비용,
재정 수수료

finance company
금융 회사

financial accounting
재무 회계

financial advertising
금융 광고

financial future
금융 선물 거래

financial institution
금융 기관

financial intermediary
금융 중개업

financial lease
금융 리스

financial management
 rate of return
 (FMRR)
재무 관리 수익율

financial market
금융시장

financial position
재정 상태, 재무 상태

financial pyramid
금융 피라미드

financial statement
재무제표

financial structure
재무구성, 자본구성

financial supermarket
금융 수퍼마켓

financing
자금조달

finder's fee
중개 수수료, 소개 수수료

finished goods
제품, 완성품

fire insurance
화재보험

firm
상사, 회사

firm commitment
전액 인수

firm offer
확정 주문

firm quote
확정 시세

first in, first out (FIFO)
선입선출법

first lien
제 1 순위 유치권, 선취권

first mortgage
제 1 저당

first-line management
제 1 선의 경영

first-year depreciation
초년도 감가상각

fiscal
재정의, 국고의, 회계의

fiscal agent
재무 대리인, 재무 대리기관

fiscal policy
재무정책, 재정정책

fiscalist
재정주의자

fixation
고정, 정착

fixed annuity
정액형 연금

fixed asset
고정 자산

fixed benefits
정액 급부

fixed charge
고정비, 확정부채

fixed cost
고정비, 고정적비용

fixed fee
고정 요금

fixed income
고정 수입, 확정 수입

fixed income statement
고정 소득 계산서

fixed premium
고정 보험료

fixed-charge coverage
고정비배율

fixed-point number
고정 소수점 수

fixed-price contract
확정 가격 계약

fixed-rate loan
고정 금리 융자

fixture
장착물, 부동산에 첨부된 동산,

flanker brand
속임수 상표

flash memory (computer)
플래시 메모리

flat
시장의 부진, 균일한

flat rate
균일요금, 정률

flat scale
정률

flat tax
일률과세, 균등세

flexible budget
변동 예산, 탄력성 예산

flexible-payment
  mortgage (FPM)
변동지불 주택융자
flextime
신축적 근로시간
flight to quality
안전투자로 자금유출
float
통화, 변동환율제도
floater
(회사설립의) 발기인,
포괄보험, 유동증권
floating currency
  exchange rate
변동통화 환율
floating debt
유동 부채
floating exchange rate
변동 환율
floating securities
유동 증권
floating supply
단기 공급품, 단기 제고품
floating-point number
부동 소수점 숫자
floating-rate note
변동 이자 부채권
flood insurance
홍수보험
floor loan
최저 융자
floor plan
평면도

floor plan insurance
담보상품보험
flotation (floatation)
  cost
발행비
flow of funds
자금 순환
flowchart
흐름도
fluctuation
(가격의)변동
fluctuation limit
변동 한계
flush (left/right)
  (computer)
플러시
follow-up letter
추가로 내는 권유장, 후속
서신
font (computer)
폰트
footing
합계, 합산
footnote
주석, 보충설명
for your information
  (FYI)
참고로
forced page break
  (computer)
강제적 페이지 구분선
forced sale
강제 매매

forced saving
강제 저축
forecasting
예측, 견적, 추정
foreclosure
차압, 유질 처분
foreign corporation
외국기업, 외국회사,
외국법인
foreign direct investment
직접 국외투자
foreign exchange
외국환, 외국환표기
단기어음
foreign income
외국 소득
foreign investment
해외 투자
foreign trade zone
외국 무역지대
forfeiture
몰수, 실권, 벌과금
forgery
위조, 변조
format (computer)
포맷
formula investing
공식을 이용한 투자
fortuitous loss
우발적 손실
forward
선물의, 앞으로

forward contract
선물 계약, 선인도 계약
forward integration
전향적 통합
forward pricing
선물 가격 매김
forward stock
선물 주식
forwarding company
운송업자
foul bill of landing
부정한 선하증권
401 (k) plan
미국기업의 연금제도
fourth market
제 4 시장
fractional share
단주
frame rate
 (computer)
프레임 비율
franchise
프랜차이즈, 가맹권
franchise tax
특별사업세,
면허세
frank
무료 배달 우편물
fraud
허위표시, 사기
fraudulent
misrepresentation
악의의 왜곡 표시

free alongside ship
  (FAS)
선측인도조건
free and clear
부동산에 저당이나
부채가 없는
free and open
  market
자유 개방시장
free enterprise
자유 기업
free market
자유 시장
free on board (FOB)
본선인도가격
free port
자유항
freehold (estate)
자유 보유권, 자유 보유
부동산
freight insurance
운임 보험
frequency
주파수
frictional unemployment
마찰적 실업
friendly suit
우호적 소송
front foot
앞면의 폭
front money
계약금, 선급금

front office
본사, 본부
frontage
정면, 전면, 임계지
front-end load
선취 수수료
frozen account
동결구좌
fulfillment
이행, 실현
full coverage
완전 적용범위
full disclosure
완전 공시
full faith and credit
완전한 신용과 신뢰
full screen display
전화면 표시
full screen display
  (computer)
전화면 표시
full-service broker
완전 서비스
fully diluted earnings per
  (common) share
완전 희석화 1 주당이익
fully paid policy
전액 지불된 보험
function key (computer)
기능키
functional authority
기능별 권한, 직능별 권한

functional obsolescence
기능적 진부화, 기능적
감가
functional organization
기능적 조직
fund accounting
기금 회계, 수지 회계
fundamental analysis
기초 분석
funded debt
장기 차입금
funded pension plan
장기 연금제

funding
적립, 기금 설립
fund-raising
자금조달
furlough
일시 휴가,
일시 해고
future interest
장래권, 미래권
futures contract
선물계약
futures market
선물시장

G

gain
이익, 이득

gain contingency
우발 이익, 우발 이득

galloping inflation
급진적 인플레이션

game card
 (computer)
게임 카드

gaming
도박

gap
격차

gap loan
갭론, 간격 대부

garnish
압류하다

garnishee
압류통고를 받은 사람,

제 3 채무자

garnishment
채권차압 통고, 채권압류

gender analysis
성별 분석

general contractor
일반 계약자, 일반 청부인

general equilibrium
 analysis
일반 균형 분석

general expense
일반비

general fund
일반 기금

general journal
일반 분개장

general ledger
원장,

총계정 원장

general liability
 insurance
종합 배상 책임보험

general lien
일반 담보권

general obligation
 bond
일반 공채

general partner
무한책임 파트너, 일반

파트너

general revenue
일반 수입

general revenue
sharing
일반 교부금

general scheme
일반적 구상

general strike
총동맹 파업

general warranty deed
일반적 담보, 책임 증서
generalist
일반직
generally accepted
  accounting principles
일반적으로 인정된 회계
원칙
generation-skipping
  transfer
세대 건너 뛴 재산 이전
generic appeal
일반적 흥미
generic bond
일반 채권
generic market
일반 시장
gentrification
(주택의) 고급화
geodemography
지구인구 통계학
gift
증여
gift deed
증여 증서
gift tax
증여세
girth
둘레, 비만
glamor stock
성장주, 인기주
glut
공급 과잉, 재고 과다

goal
목표, 최종 목표
goal congruence
목표 일치
goal programming
목표 계획법(몇개의
대립되는 목표 허용)
goal setting
목표 설정
go-between
중개자
going long
증권이나 채권의 구매
going private
주식의 비공개
going public
주식의 공개,주식의 상장
going short
소유하지 않는 증권의
매각
going-concern
  value
계속 기업의 가치
gold fixing
금 가격, 금의 가치 결정
gold mutual fund
금광 채굴회사 투자 신탁
gold standard
금본위제
goldbrick
가짜 금덩어리,
모조품

goldbug
금본위제 지지자, 황금광

golden handcuffs
소유자의 업무 집행
조건의 기업 매수

golden handshake
(고액의) 퇴직금

golden parachute
고액의 퇴직 수당 지불
보증 고용 계약

good delivery
증권의 적격 조달

good faith
성실

good money
고임금

good title
저당없는 좋은 권리증

good-faith deposit
계약 공탁금

goodness-of-fit test
적합도 검정

goods
재화, 재물, 상품

goods and services
상품과 서비스

good-till-canceled order (GTC)
취소할 때까지 유효한
주문

goodwill
영업권

grace period
유예 기간

graduated lease
임대료 누진형 리스

graduated payment mortgage (GPM)
누진 반제방식 저당

graduated wage
누진식 임금

graft
부당 이득

grandfather clause
조부 조항

grant
보조(금), 수여

grantee
양수인

grantor
교부자

grantor trust
증여 신탁

graph
표, 도표

graph *(computer)*
그래프

graphics card *(computer)*
그래픽 카드

gratis
무료로

gratuitous
무료의, 무상의

gratuity
팁, 선물

graveyard market
묘지 시장, 계속적인 하락
시장

graveyard shift
심야 근무

gray scale *(computer)*
그레이 스케일

great depression
대공항

greenmail
그린메일, 주식매점

gross
전체의, 총액의

gross amount
총액

gross billing
총액 청구

gross earnings
총 수입, 총 수익

gross estate
총 유산액

gross income
총 소득, 총 수입

gross lease
총 임대계약 지역

gross leaseable area
비용 차주 부담의 임대
계약

gross national debt
국민 총부채

gross national expenditure
국민 총소비

gross national product
 (GNP)
국민 총생산

gross profit
총 이익

gross profit method
총 이익법

gross profit ratio
총 이익률

gross rating point
 (GRP)
총 시청율

gross rent multiplier
 GRM)
총 임대료 승수

gross revenue
총 수입

gross ton
영국 톤(2240 파운드)

gross weight
총 중량

ground lease
토지 임대

ground rent
땅세, 지대

group credit insurance
단체 신용보험

group disability insurance
단체 상해보험

group health insurance
단체 건강보험

group life insurance
단체 생명보험

growing-equity mortgage (GEM)
지분 성장 담보

growth fund
성장형 투자 신탁

growth rate
성장율, 증가율

growth stock
성장주

guarantee
담보

guarantee of signature
서명 보증

guaranteed annual wage (GAW)
연간 보장 임금

guaranteed bond
보증부 사채

guaranteed income contract (GIC)
소득 보장 계약

guaranteed insurability
보증 피보험성

guaranteed letter
보증서

guaranteed mortgage
보증 담보

guaranteed security
보증 증권

guarantor
보증인

guaranty
보증, 보증 계약, 담보, 보증인

guardian
후견인

guardian deed
후견인 날인증서

guideline lives
감가상각 수명

guild
동업조합

H

habendum
물건 표시 조례
hacker
해커, 컴퓨터광
half duplex
반이중 방식
half-life
반감기
halo effect
후광 효과
hammering the
  market
집중적인 주식의 매도
handling allowance
취급비
hangout
소굴, 집합소
hard cash
경화, 현금
hard currency
경화, 교환 가능 통화
hard disk (computer)
하드 디스크
hard dollars
실제로 지불한 현금
hard drive (computer)
하드 디스크 장치
hard goods
내구 소비제

hard money
경화, 현금
hard return (computer)
확실한 복귀
hardware (computer)
하드웨어
hardwired (computer)
배선에의해 접속된
hash total
해시 합계
hatch (computer)
고안해내다
hazard insurance
위험보험
head and shoulders
주식 가격 하락 패턴
head of household
세대주
header (computer)
헤더
headhunter
인재 스카우트 담당자
health maintenance
  organization (HMO)
건강관리 기관
hearing
청문회, 공청회
heavy industry
중공업

hectare
헥타르
hedge
(손실, 위험에 대한)
방지책
heirs
(유언이 없었을 때) 상속인
heirs and assigns
상속인과 양수인
help index *(computer)*
도움 인덱스
help screen *(computer)*
도움 화면
help wizard *(computer)*
도움 마법사
heterogeneous
이질의
heuristic
발견적, 발견적 방법
hidden agenda
숨겨진 의도
hidden asset
감춰진 자산
hidden inflation
숨겨진 인플레이션
hidden tax
숨겨진 세금
hierarchy
계층구조
high credit
높은 신용도
high flyer
고가의 투기주

high resolution
(computer)
고해상도
high technology
첨단 기술
highest and best
use
최고 최선의 사용
high-grade bond
우량채권
high-involvement
model
깊이 연류된 모델
highlight
(computer)
하이라이트
highs
상한가
high-speed
(computer)
고속도
high-tech stock
하이텍 주
historical
cost
실제 원가
historical
structure
역사적 구조물, 역사적
조직
historical yield
역사적 생산고
hit list
판매 대상자 명단

hit the bricks
종업원이 파업을
시작하다

hobby loss
취미에의한 손실

hold harmless clause
배상책임 면제 합의

holdback
방해, 지연, 보관물

holdback pay
지불보류 임금

holder in due course
정당 소지인

holder of record
기록 보유자

hold-harmless agreements
배상책임 면제조항

holding
보유, 소유

holding company
지주 회사

holding fee
보유 수수료

holding period
보유 기간

holdover tenant
보유 기간 만기후 점유자

home key
 (computer)
홈 키

home page (computer)
홈 페이지

homeowner warranty
 program (how)
주택소유자 보증
프로그램

homeowner's association
주택 소유자 협회

homeowner's equity
account
주택 소유자 지분 계정

homeowner's policy
주택 소유자 보험

homestead
(부속 건물이 있는) 주택

homestead tax exemption
부동산세 면제

homogeneous
동질의

homogeneous oligopoly
동질적 과점

honor
명예

honorarium
사례금

horizontal analysis
수평적 분석

horizontal channel
integration
수평적 계통 통합 (경쟁자
포함)

horizontal combination
수평적 결합

horizontal expansion
수평적 확장

horizontal merger
수평적 합병

horizontal specialization
수평적 특소화

horizontal union
수평적 단결

host computer *(computer)*
호스트 컴퓨터, 대용량
컴퓨터

hot cargo
밀수화물

hot issue
주목된 문제, 인기있는
신주

hot stock
인기주

house
집, 주택

house account
사내 계정

house to house
가가호호, 집집마다

house-to-house sampling
가가호호 샘플링

house-to-house selling
가정 방문 판메

housing bond
주택 채권

housing code
주택 기준법규

housing starts
주택 착공건수

huckster
행상인, 광고업자, 강매인

human factors
인적 요소

human relations
인간 관계

human resource
 accounting
인적 자원 회계

human resources
인적 자원

human resources
 management
 (HRM)
인적자원 관리

hurdle rate
투자의 기대 수익률

hush money
무마비, 입막음 돈

hybrid annuity
복합형 연금

hyperinflation
초인플레이션

hyperlink *(computer)*
하이퍼 링크

hypertext
하이퍼텍스트

hypothecate
담보에 넣다

hypothesis
가정, 가설

hypothesis testing
가설 검정

I

icon
아이콘

ideal capacity
이상적 조업도

idle capacity
유휴 생산능력

illegal dividend
불법 배당

illiquid
비유동적인, (기업의)
현금부족

image
  (computer)
이미지

image advertising
이미지 광고

image definition
  (computer)
이미지 해상력

image file
  (computer)
이미지 파일

impacted area
충격을 받은 지역,
인구급증 지역

impaired capital
손상 자본

impasse
곤경, 난국

imperfect market
불완전 시장

imperialism
제국주의

implied
은연중의,
암시적인

implied contract
묵시 계약

implied easement
묵시적 지역권

implied in fact
contract
묵시적 실제 계약

implied warranty
묵시적 보증,
묵시적 담보

import
수입(하다)

import quota
수입 할당

imposition
과세, 세금, 부과

impound
(물건을) 몰수하다,
압수하다

impound account
몰수계좌

imprest fund, imprest system
정액 전도 자금, 정액 전도 제도

improved land
개량된 토지

improvement
개량, 증축

improvements and betterments insurance
설비 개량 보험

imputed cost
부가 원가,
재재 원가

imputed income
귀속 소득

imputed interest
귀속 이자

imputed value or imputed income
귀속 가치 또는 귀속 소득

in perpetuity
영구히

in the money
재정적으로 성공한,
부유한

in the tank
시가의 폭락

inactive stock or inactive bond
비인기 주 또는 비인기 채권

inadvertently
부주의로

incapacity
무능력

incentive fee
장려 보수

incentive pay
장려금

incentive stock option (ISO)
자사주 장려 구입권

incentive wage plan
장려 임금제

inchoate
미종결의, 미완료의

incidental damages
우발적 손해 배상금

income
이익, 소득

income accounts
손익계산서

income approach
손익법, 수익환원법,
수익방식

income averaging
소득 평준화

income bond
수익 사채

income effect
소득 효과

income group
소득층, 소득계층

income in respect of a
  decedent
사망자 분의 소득
income property
수익 재산
income redistribution
소득 재분배
income replacement
대체소득
income splitting
소득 분활법
income statement
손익계산서
income stream
소득계산서, 손익계산서
income tax
소득세, 법인세,
법인소득세
income tax return
소득세 신고서, 법인세
신고서
incompatible
호환성이 없는
incompatible
  (computer)
호환성이 없는
incompetent
무능력의, 무자격자
incontestable clause
(보험의) 불가쟁 조항
inconvertible money
불환지폐

incorporate
주식회사로하다, 법인
조직으로 하다
incorporation
회사,
회사설립
incorporeal property
무체 재산
incremental analysis
증분 분석
incremental cash flow
증분 캐시플로
(현금 유통)
incremental spending
증분 지출
incurable depreciation
교정불능 감가상각
indemnify
보상하다
indemnity
손해배상
indent
(computer)
들여쓰기
indenture
신탁계약서
independence
독립(성)
independent adjuster
독립 조정인, 독립 손해
조정인

independent contractor
독립적 도급인,
독립계약자
independent store
독립 점포(상점)
independent union
독립 노동조합
independent
  variables
독립변수
indeterminate premium
  life insurance
불확정 보험료 생명보험
index
지수(예 Standard & Poor),
색인, 지표
index basis
지수 기준
index fund
지표채,
지표 지금(자금)
index lease
지수에 따라 렌트비가
변동되는 리스
index options
주식 지수 옵션
indexation
지수법
indexed life
  insurance
지수에 따라 보험료가
변동되는 보험

indexed loan
지수에 따라 변동되는
장기 대부
indexing
지수법, 지수화, 색인첨부
indirect cost
간접비
indirect labor
간접 노동
indirect overhead
간접 경비
indirect production
간접 생산
individual bargaining
개별 교섭
individual life
  insurance
개인 생명보험
individual retirement
account (IRA)
개인 퇴직금 구좌
inductive reasoning
귀납적 추리
industrial
산업(상)의,
공업(상)의
industrial advertising
산업 광고
industrial consumer
산업 제품 소비자
industrial engineer
산업 기사(엔지니어)

industrial fatigue
산업적 피로
industrial goods
생산재
industrial park
공업 단지
industrial production
공업생산(액)
industrial property
공업 소유권
industrial psychology
산업심리학
industrial relations
노사관계
industrial revolution
산업혁명
industrial union
산업별 노동조합
industrialist
기업가, 실업가,
생산업자
industry
업종, 산업
industry standard
산업 기준
inefficiency in the market
시장의 비능률
infant industry argument
유아산업 주장
inferential statistics
추론적 통계

inferior good
하등품, 열등품
inferred authority
추정된 권위
inflation
인플레이션
inflation accounting
인플레이션 회계,
화폐가치 변동 회계
inflation endorsement
인플레이션 배서, 건설
단가 상승을 적용
inflation rate
물가 상승률
inflationary gap
인플레이션 갭
inflationary spiral
악성 인플레이션
informal leader
비공식 지도자
information flow
정보의 흐름,
정보 유통
information flow (computer)
정보의 흐름,
정보 유통
information page
정보 페이지
information page (computer)
정보 페이지

information return
정보 복귀

infrastructure
하부 조직

infringement
침해, 위반

ingress and egress
출입 할 수있는 권리

inherent explosion clause
(보험의) 폭발 위험 조항
포함

inherit
상속하다

inheritance
상속

inheritance tax
상속세

in-house
구내

initial public offering (IPO)
신규 상장, 최초의 공모

initiative
주도, 독창력

injuction
금지, 금지명령

injuction bond
금지 명령 채무 증서

injury independent of all other means
이전 상해는 포함하지 않는 상해를 적용하는 건강보험

inland carrier
내륙 운송업자

inner city
도심(부)

innovation
혁신, 일신

input
투입, 제공

input *(computer)*
입력

input field *(computer)*
입력 필드

input mask *(computer)*
입력 마스크

input-output device *(computer)*
입출력 장치

inside information
내부 정보

inside lot
내부 부지, 내부 분양지

insider
내부자, 내부인

insolvency
지불 불능

insolvency clause
채무 초과 조항

inspection
실사, 검사, 조사

installation *(computer)*
설치

installment
분할 불입

installment contract
할부 계약

installment sale
월부 판매

institutional investor
기관 투자가

institutional
  lender
대출기관

instrument
증서, 문서, 수단

instrumentalities of
  transportation
수송 수단, 수송 방법

instrumentality
도구, 수단

insurability
보험 적합성

insurable interest
피보험 이익

insurable title
보험 가능 권리증서

insurance
보험

insurance company
  (insurer)
보험회사 (보험자)

insurance contract
보험 계약,

insurance coverage
보험 보상 범위

insurance settlement
보험금 해결, 보험금 결제

insure
보험에 들다, 보증하다

insured
보험 계약자, 피보험자

insured account
보험 보상범위에 포함된
구좌

insurgent
폭도, 반란자

intangible asset
무형 자산

intangible reward
무형의 보수

intangible value
무형의 가치

integrated circuit
직접회로, 통합회로

integration, backward
후방적 통합

integration, forward
전방적 통합

integration, horizontal
수평적 통합

integration, vertical
수직적 통합

integrity
완전성, 보증

interactive
서로 작용하는

interactive
  (computer)
대화식의

interactive system
대화형 시스템
interest
이자, 이자율, 이해관계
interest group
이해관계자 집단
interest rate
이자율
interest sensitive policies
금리 연동방식 보험증권
interest-only loan
(원금 만기일까지) 이자만
지불하는 대부
interface
경계면, 인터페이스
interim audit
기중 감사, 연락
interim financing
중간 자금조달
interim statement
중간 계산서
**interindustry
  competition**
산업간 경쟁
**interlocking
  directorate**
겸직 임원제도
interlocutory decree
중간 판결, 잠정적 판결
intermediary
중재인, 중개, 중간물
intermediate goods
중간재

intermediate term
중간 기간
intermediation
중개, 매개
intermittent production
때때로 중단되는 생산
internal audit
내부 감사
internal check
내부 견제
internal control
내부 통제
internal expansion
내부 확장
internal financing
내부 자금 조달
internal memory
내부 기억장치
**internal memory
  (computer)**
내장 메모리
**internal modem
  (computer)**
내장 모뎀
**internal rate of return
  (IRR)**
내부 이익율, 내부 수익율
**Internal Revenue Service
  (IRS)**
국세청
**International Bank for
  Reconstruction and
  Development**
국제부흥개발은행

89

international cartel
국제적 카르텔, 국제적
기업연합
international law
국제법
International Monetary
Fund (IMF)
국제통화기금 (IMF)
International Monetary
Market (IMM)
국제 통화 시장
international union
국제적 연맹
internet
인터넷
internet protocol (IP)
address
인터넷 규약 주소
internet service provider
인터넷 서비스 공급자
interperiod income tax
allocation
연간 사이의 소득세 배당
interpleader
경합 권리자 확정 수속
interpolation
삽입, 기입
interpreter
통역, 통역자
interrogatories
질문, 질문서
interval scale
단위 척도

interview
회견, 면접
interview, structured
공식적 면접
interview, unstructured
비공식적 면접
interviewer basis
면접인 기준
intraperiod tax allocation
세금의 기간내 배분
intrinsic value
내재 가치
inventory
재고 자산, 상품 목록
inventory certificate
재고 증명서
inventory control
재고 관리
inventory financing
재고품 금융
inventory planning
재고 계획
inventory shortage
(shrinkage)
재고부족(감소)
inventory turnover
재고 자산 회전율
inverse condemnation
(정부의) 재산 수용에 대한
보상
inverted yield curve
반전된 이자 산출 곡선

invest
투자하다
investment
투자, 투자 자산
investment advisory
service
투자 자문 서비스
investment banker
투자 금융업자
investment club
투자 클럽
investment company
투자 회사, 투자 신탁회사
investment counsel
투자 상담
investment grade
투자 등급
investment interest
expense
투자이자 비용
investment life cycle
투자 수명
investment strategy
투자 전략
investment trust
투자신탁
investor relations
department
투자가 관계 담당과
invoice
송장
involuntary conversion
비자발적 전환

involuntary lien
강제 유치권
involuntary trust
강제 신탁
involuntary
 unemployment
비자발적 실업
Inwood annuity factor
인우드 연금율
iota
소량, 미량
irregulars
같지 않은 상품
irreparable harm,
 irreparable damage
회복할 수 없는 손해,
회복할 수 없는 피해
irretrievable
회복할 수 없는
irretrievable
 (computer)
회복할 수 없는
irrevocable
취소할 수없는
irrevocable
 trust
철회 불능 신탁
issue
발행물, 문제
issued and outstanding
발행되고 공모하는 주식
issuer
발행자

itemized
  deductions
항목별 공제

iteration
반복

itinerant worker
이동 노동자

J

jawboning
강제적 설득, 강제적 권고

J-curve
제이 커브

job
일, 직업, 기능

job bank
직업 소개 은행

job classification
직무 분류

job cost sheet
제조 지시서별 원가
계산표

job depth
작업 심도

job description
직무 기술서

job evaluation
직무 평가

job jumper
직장을 자주 바꾸는 사람

job lot
싸구려 물건

job order
제조 지시서,
업무 지시

job placement
직업 소개

job rotation
직무 순환

job satisfaction
직무 만족

job security
직업 안정

job sharing
일감 나누기

job shop
하청 생산 공장

job specification
작업 지시 명세서

job ticket
작업 시간표

jobber
중매업자,
중개업자

joint account
공동 계좌, 공동 구좌

**joint and several
  liability**
연대적 채무

**joint and survivor
  annuity**
공동 생존자 연금

joint fare, joint rate
결합 운임, 결합 비율

joint liability
공동 채무, 연대 책임

joint product cost
결합 원가
joint return
공동 신고
joint stock company
공동 주식회사
joint tendency
공동 소유
joint venture
공동 출자 사업, 합작투자
jointly and severally
연대적 책임
journal
분개장, 거래기록
journal entry
분개장 입력
journal voucher
분개 증빙, 분개 전표
journalize
분개장에 써넣다
journeyman
장인, 기능인
judgment
판단, 판결
judgment creditor
판결 채권자
judgment debtor
판결 채무
judgment lien
판결 선취권
judgment proof
판정 증명
judgment sample
평가 견본

judicial bond
판결 보장
judicial foreclosure or
  judicial sale
사법상의
jumbo certificate of
  deposit
큰 금액 예금증서
junior issue
하위 증권
junior lien
후순위 선취특권
junior mortgage
후순위 저당
junior partner
하급 사원,
하급 파트너
junior security
하위 증권
junk bond
위험도가 높은 값 싼 증권
jurisdiction
재판권, 관할권,
관할구역
jurisprudence
법률학, 법리학
jury
배심
just compensation
정당한 보상
justifiable
정당한
justified price
정당한 가격

K

Keogh plan
키오 플랜

key *(computer)*
키

key person life and health insurance
경영자 보험, 기업 간부 보험

key-area evaluation
중요한 지역 평가

keyboard *(computer)*
키보드

kickback
부당 수수료, 뇌물

kicker
추가적 특권

kiddie tax
14세 미만자 불로소득 세금

killing
큰 보상

kiting
융통 어음 사용

know-how
노하우, 기술지식

knowledge intensive
지식 집중적인

know-your-customer rule
고객을 알아야하는 법칙

kudos
명성, 영광

L

labeling laws
라벨 표시법
labor
노동, 노동자
labor agreement
노동 협약
labor dispute
노동 쟁의
labor force
노동력,
노동 인구
labor intensive
노동 집약적인
labor mobility
노동 이동성
labor piracy
노동자 쟁탈
labor pool
노동력 출처
labor union
노동조합
laches
권리를 행사하는 청구가
늦음
lading
선적
lagging indicator
지행 지표

LAN (local area
  network) *(computer)*
구내 정보통신망
land
토지
land banking
토지 저당 대출 은행업
land contract
토지 사용 계약
land development
토지 개발
land trust
토지 신탁
landlocked
육지로 둘러싸인
landlord
집주인, 지주
landmark
경계표, 역사적 건조물
landscape (format)
  (computer)
세로 방향
land-use intensity
토지 이용 집약도
land-use planning
토지 이용 계획
land-use
  regulation
토지 이용 규제

land-use
  succession
토지 이용 상속

lapping
외상 매출금 회수 시간
차이를 이용한 부정 행위

lapse
(보험 계약의) 실효

lapsing schedule
고정자산 증감 명세표

last in, last out (LIFO)
후입 선출법

last sale
최근의 주식 판매

latent defect
잠재 하자

latitude
위도, 허용 범위

law
법, 법률, 법령

law of diminishing returns
생산 증가 감소의 법칙

law of increasing costs
생산비 증가의 법칙

law of large numbers
대수의 법칙

law of supply and demand
공급과 수요의 법칙

lay off
일시 해고

lead time
준비 시간

leader
지도자, 지휘자

leader pricing
고객 유인 가격 결정

leading indicators
선행 지수, 선행 지표

lease
리스 계약, 임대차 계약

lease with option to
  purchase
구매 선택권을 포함한
임대

leasehold
임차권, 정기 임대차권

leasehold improvement
리스 물건 개량비

leasehold insurance
임대 보험

leasehold mortgage
임대 저당, 임대저당권

leasehold value
임대 가치

least-effort
  principle
최소 노력의 원리

leave of absence
휴직 (휴가, 휴학)의 허가,
무보수 휴가

ledger
원장

legal entity
법적 실체

legal investment
법적 투자

legal list
법적 투자 종목

legal monopoly
합법적 독점

legal name
정식 이름

legal notice
적법성의 통지

legal opinion
법률 전문가의 의견

legal right
법적 권리

legal tender
법적 통화

legal wrong
법적 부정

legatee
유산 수령인

lender
빌려주는 사람, 여신자

less than carload
 (L/C)
화차 한 대 분보다 적은
중량

lessee
임차인

lessor
임대인

letter of intent
계약 의도 표명서

letter stock
비등록주

level debt service
부채 균등화 서비스

level out
균등화, 균일화

level premium
평준 보험료

level-payment income
 stream
정액 연금의 정기적 지불

level-payment
 mortgage
정액 지불 저당

leverage
차입 효과, 영향력

leveraged buyout (LBO)
기업 담보 차입 매수

leveraged company
차입 자본을 이용하는
기업

leveraged lease
차입 자본을 이용하는
리스

levy
압류

liability
부채, 채무

liability dividend
책임 배당

liability insurance
책임보험

liability, business exposures
사업의 경제적 손해에 대한 책임

liability, civil
민사 책임

liability, criminal
형사 책임

liability, legal
법정 책임

liability, professional
전문 직업자의 책임

liable
법률상의 책임

libel
문서 비방죄

license
면허, (특허의) 사용권

license bond
면허 허가 채권

license law
면허법

licensee
인가받은 사람, 면허, 면허 시험

lien
리엔, 담보권, 선취특권

life cycle
생활 주기, 생애 주기

life estate
종신 부동산권, 종신 물건

life expectancy
기대 여명

life tenant
종신 부동산권자

lighterage
거룻배 운반, 거룻배 사용료

like-kind property
동종류의 재산

limit order
가격 지정 주문

limit up, limit down
일일 가격 변동 한계

limited audit
한정 감사

limited company
유한책임회사

limited distribution
한정 분배

limited liability
유한책임, 한정책임

limited occupancy agreement
한정된 주거의 합의

limited or special partner
유한책임 사원

limited partnership
유한 파트너쉽

limited payment life insurance
유한지불 생명보험

line
명령 계통
line and staff
  organization
직계 참모조직
line authority
라인 권한
line control
라인 관리, 라인 제어
line extension
라인 확장
line function
라인 기능
line management
라인 관리
line of credit
신용 한도
line organization
라인 조직
line pitch
  (computer)
행간격
line printer
라인 프린터
link *(computer)*
연결
linked object
상호 연결된 물체
linked object
  (computer)
연결 객체
liquid asset
당좌 자산

liquid crystal display
  (LCD) *(computer)*
액정 디스플레이
liquidate
청산하다, 정리하다,
해산하다
liquidated damages
확정 배상액
liquidated debt
확정 채무
liquidated value
청산 금액
liquidation
청산
liquidation dividend
청산 배당
liquidity
유동성
liquidity preference
유동성 선호
liquidity ratio
유동성 비율
list
계열, 목록, 명부
list price
표시가격
listed options
상장된 옵션
listed security
상장된 유가증권
listing
상장

listing agent, listing broker
부동산을 취급물건
장부에 올린
부동산업자(브로커)

listing requirements
상장 요건

litigant
소송 당사자

litigation
소송

living trust
생전 신탁

load
짐, 적재하다

load fund
수수료 부가 펀드

loan
대출금, 대출, 차입금, 여신

loan application
대출 신청서

loan committee
대출 위원회

loan value
대출 가치

loan-to-value ratio (LTV)
평가가격 융자율

lobbyist
로비스트

lock box
사서함

locked in
고정된, 변경할 수 없는

lockout
공장폐쇄, 축출

lock-up option
(자본의) 고정

log in (log on) *(computer)*
로그인

log off *(computer)*
로그아웃

logic diagram
논리도

logic diagram *(computer)*
논리 다이아그램

login identification (login ID) *(computer)*
로그인 아이디

logo
로고

long bond
장기채권

long coupon
장기 이자표

long position
상승 기대주를 매입

longevity pay
연공 가급

long-range planning
장기 계획

long-term debt or long-term liability
장기 부채

long-term gain (loss)
장기 수익(손실)

long-term trend
장기적 경향

long-wave cycle
장기 파동 순환

loop
루프, 순환

loophole
법을 빠져나갈 수단

loose rein
통제의 완화

loss
손실, 차손, 손해

loss adjustment
손해 조정

loss carryback
결손금의 소급

loss carryforward
결손금의 이월

loss contingency
우발적 손실

loss leader
저가 상품, 특저가품

loss of income insurance
소득 손실 보험

loss ratio
손해율

lot and block
로트와 블록의 필지
인식방법

lot line
용지 변경선

lotter
복권

low
낮은

low resolution
  (computer)
저해상도

lower case character/letter
  (computer)
소문자

lower of cost or
  market
재고의 장부 가격이 시장
가격보다 낮음

lower-involvement
  model
저연루 광고효과 모델

low-grade
저등급, 저품위

low-tech
저수준 공업기술

lump sum
일괄 지불 총액

lumpsum distribution
일괄 분배

lump-sum
  purchase
일괄 구입

luxury tax
사치세

M

macro *(computer)*
마크로
macroeconomics
거시경제학
macroenvironment
거시적 환경
magnetic card *(computer)*
자기 카드
magnetic strip
 (computer)
자기대
mail fraud
우편물 사기
mailbox *(computer)*
편지상자, 메일박스
mailing list
우편 수취자 명단
main menu *(computer)*
주 메뉴, 메인 메뉴
mainframe *(computer)*
대형 범용컴퓨터, 메인
프레임
maintenance
보수, 보전, 유지, 부양
maintenance
 bond
부양 보증
maintenance fee
유지비, 관리비

maintenance method
유지 방법
majority
다수결, 과반수
majority shareholder
지배 주주
maker
제조업자
make-work
(노동자의 실직
대책으로서 시키는 임시)
일 또는 고용
malicious mischief
고의의 기물 손괴
malingerer
꾀병을 부리는 사람
malingering
꾀병을 부리다
mall
쇼핑 몰
malpractice
직무상 과실, 의료과오
manage
경영하다, 관리하다
managed account
관리 회계
managed currency
관리 통화

managed economy
통제 경제
management
경영, 관리
management agreement
경영 계약
management audit
경영 감사
management by
crisis
위기에 의한 관리
management by exception
예외에 기준한 관리
management by objective
 (MBO)
목적에 의한 관리
management by walking
around (MBWA)
시찰 안내형 경영
management consultant
경영 자문
management cycle
경영 주기
management fee
증권, 투자물 관리비,
부동산 관리 수수료
management game
경영 게임, 관리 게임
management guide
운영방침 안내 책자
management information
 system (MIS)
경영 정보 시스템

management prerogative
경영자 특권
management ratio
경영 비율
management science
경영 과학
management style
경영 스타일
management system
경영 시스템, 관리 시스템
manager
경영자, 관리자, 부장
managerial accounting
관리 회계
managerial grid
관리 격자도
mandate
명령, 위임
mandatory copy
강제적 복사
man-hour
1 인의 1 시간 생산성
manifest
적하 목록, 선언, 성명서
manipulation
시장 조작, 조종
manual
취급 설명서, 수동 조작의
manual skill
수공 기술
manufacture
제조, 생산

manufacturing cost
제조 원가, 제조비
manufacturing inventory
제조용 재고품
manufacturing order
제조 지시서, 생산 주문
map
지도
margin
차익, 이익, 위탁 증거금,
한계
margin account
증거금 계정
margin call
마진콜,
추가 증거금 청구
margin of profit
채산
margin of safety
안전 한계
marginal cost
한계 원가, 한계 비용
marginal cost curve
한계 비용 곡선
marginal efficiency of capital
자본의 한계 효율
marginal producer
한계 생산자
marginal propensity to consume (MPC)
한계 소비 성향

marginal propensity to invest
한계 투자 성향
marginal propensity to save (MPS)
한계 저축 성향
marginal property
한계 재산, 한계 부동산
marginal revenue
한계 수입
marginal tax rate
한계 세율
marginal utility
한계 효용
margins
이윤폭, 이윤 차액, 증거금
marital deduction
부부 공제
mark to the market
시가 기준 유가증권 자산
평가
markdown
가격 인하
market
마켓, 시장
market aggregation
시장 합산
market analysis
시장 분석
market area
시장 지역

market basket
마켓 바스켓, 시장 바구니
market comparison
approach
시장 비교 수법
market demand
시장 수요
market development
index
시장 개발 지수
market economy
시장 경제
market equilibrium
시장 균형
market index
시장 지수
market letter
시장 안내(서)
market order
시가 인수 주문
market penetration
시장 침투
market price
시장 가격, 시가
market rent
시가 임대
market research
시장 조사
market segmentation
시장 세분화
market share
시장 점유율

market system
시장주직, 시장 시스템
market test
시장 점검
market timing
시장 시기 맞추기
market value
시가, 시장 가격
market value clause
시장 가격 조항
marketability
시장성
marketable securities
시장성이 있는 유가증권
marketable title
매매할 수 있는 증서
marketing
마케팅, 시장 거래
marketing concept
마케팅 개념, 마케팅 발상
marketing director
시장 담당 이사
marketing information
system
마케팅 정보 시스템
marketing mix
마케팅 믹스
marketing plan
마케팅 계획
marketing research
시장 조사
markup
가격 인상, 이윤폭

marriage penalty	matching principle
결혼 벌금	(비용, 수익의) 대응 원칙
Marxism	material
마르크스주의	재료, 자료, 원료
mask *(computer)*	material fact
마스크	중요한 사실
mass appeal	material man
대중의 흥미를 끌다	자재 공급업자
mass communication	materiality
대중 전달,	중요성
매스컴	materials handling
mass media	자재 취급
매스 미디어, 대중전달	materials management
매체	원재료 관리
mass production	matrix
대량생산	행렬, 주형
master boot record	matrix organization
(computer)	매트릭스 조직
MBR, 매스터 부트 섹터	mature economy
master lease	성숙한 경제
기본 임차권	matured endowment
master limited	양로 자금
partnership	maturity
기본 유한회사	성숙, 만기
master plan	maturity date
마스터 플랜, 종합 계획	만기일, 지불 기일
master policy	maximize *(computer)*
일괄 보험증권	극대화하다
master-servant rule	maximum capacity
고용 규칙	최대 능력, 생산 능력
masthead	MCAT
발행인 난, 돛대 꼭대기	지방 무이자 할인채

mean return
평균 이익
mean, arithmetric
산술 평균
mean, geometric
기하 평균
mechanic's lien
건설업자의 담보권
mechanization
기계화
media
매체, 수단, 방편
media buy
매체 구매
media buyer
매체 구매 담당자
media plan
매체 계획
media planner
매체 계획자
media player *(computer)*
미디어 플레이어
media weight
미디어 전달량
mediation
중재, 주선, 조정
medical examination
건강 진단, 신체 검사
medium
중간물, 매체, 수단
medium of exchange
교환수단

medium-term bond
중기채권
meeting of the minds
의견의 일치, 합의
megabucks
100 만 달러, 거액의 돈
megabyte
메가바이트
member bank
회원 은행
member firm or member corporation
회원 회사
memorandum
비망록, 각서, 정관, 기본정관
memory *(computer)*
메모리, 기억장치
menial
시시한, 천한
menu bar *(computer)*
메뉴 바
mercantile
상인의, 상업의
mercantile agency
상사 대리점, 상업 흥신소
mercantile law
상법, 상업법
mercantilism
중상주의
merchandise
상품, 제품

merchandise allowance
상품 준비금, 상품 공제

merchandise broker
상품 중개업자

merchandise control
상품 관리, 상품 통제

merchandising
상품화 계획, 유통업

merchandising director
상품화 계획 담당자

merchandising service
상품화 서비스

merchant bank
투자은행, 증권 인수은행,
상인은행

merchantable
시장성이 있는

merge
합병하다, 결합하다

merger
합병, 기업 결합

merit increase
능률제 승급

merit rating
인사고과, 근무평정

metes and bounds
경계, 경계선

methods-time
  measurement (MTM)
시간 측정 방법

metric system
미터법

metrication
미터법화

metropolitan area
대도시권

microeconomics
미시적 경제학

micromotion study
미세동작 연구

midcareer plateau
경력의 정체 상태

middle management
중간 관리자,
중간 관리층

midnight deadline
한밤중의 최종기한

migrate
  (computer)
이동하다

migratory worker
계절 노동자

military-industrial
  complex
군과산업 집합체

milking
우유 짜기, 최대의 이익
만들기

milking strategy
최대의 이익 만들기 전략

millage rate
마일당 비율

millionaire
백만장자, 큰 부자

millionaire on paper
서류상 백만장자,
명목상 백만장자

mineral rights
채굴권

minimax principle
미니맥스 원리

minimize
  (computer)
최소화하다

minimum lease
  payments
최소 리스 지불

minimum lot area
최소 구획지역

minimum pension
  liability
최저 연금채무

minimum premium
  deposit plan
최저 보험료 공탁금 방식

minimum wage
최저 임금

minor
미성년자, 소수의

minority interest or
  minority investment
소액주주 지분 또는
소액주주 투자

mintage
화폐 주조

minutes
의사록

misdemeanor
경범죄, 비행

mismanagement
잘못된 관리

misrepresentation
부실 표시, 허위 진술

misstatement of age
나이의 허위기재

mistake
오류, 착오

mistake of law
법률의 착오

mitigation of damages
손해 배상의 완화

mix
혼합

mixed economy
혼합 경제

mixed perils
혼합 위험

mixed signals
혼합 신호,
알쏭달쏭

mode
방법, 양식

model unit
모델 유니트,
모델장치

modeling
모형 제작

modeling language
모델링 언어

modern portfolio theory (MPT)
현대적 증권일람표 이론
modified accrual
수정 발생
modified life insurance
수정된생명보험
modified union shop
수정된 노조 기업체 (고용 조건이 노사 협정으로 정해지는 기업)
module (computer)
모듈
mom and pop store
소규모 소매점, 부부 경영 상점
momentum
추진력, 여세, 운동량
monetarist
화폐주의자
monetary
화폐의, 통화의
monetary item
금전 항목
monetary reserve
통화 준비금
monetary standard
통화 기준
money
화폐, 금전, 통화
money illusion
화폐 가치 착각

money income
화폐 소득
money market
(단기) 금융시장
money market fund
단기 금융상품 투자신탁
money supply
화폐 공급량, 통화 공급량
monopolist
독점자
monopoly
독점, 독점 기업
monopoly price
독점 가격
monopsony
수요 독점, 구매자 독점
monthly compounding of interest
매월 복리 계산 이자
monthly investment plan
매월 일정 금액 투자 계획
month-to-month tenancy
월세차용
monument
기념 건조물
moonlighting
(야간의) 부업
moral hazard
도덕적 해이, 도덕적 위험
moral law
도덕률

moral obligation bond
도덕적 지불보증 채권
moral suasion
도덕적 권고
morale
사기, 의욕, 도덕, 도의
moratorium
지불유예, 지불정지
mortality table
(연령별) 사망율 통계표
mortgage
저당, 저당권
mortgage assumption
저당권 인수
mortgage banker
저당은행
mortgage bond
담보부 채권
mortgage broker
저당권 중개인
mortgage commitment
저당권 매매 약정
mortgage constant
저당비율 상수
mortgage correspondent
저당권 중개인
mortgage debt
저당채무, 담보 채무
mortgage discount
저당 할인
mortgage insurance
저당 보험

mortgage insurance policy
저당보험 증서, 저당보험
계약
mortgage lien
저당 선취권
mortgage out
개발업자의 건설 단가
초과 대출
mortgage relief
저당제거
mortgage servicing
저당 서비스 제공
mortgage-backed
  certificate
담보부 증서
mortgage-backed security
담보부 유가증권
mortgagee
저당권자, 저당 채권자
mortgagor
양도 저당권 설정자, 저당
채무자
motion study
동작연구
motivation
동기, 동기 부여
motor freight
자동차 화물
mouse (computer)
마우스
mouse pad (computer)
마우스 패드

movement
운동, 동향

mover and shaker
실력자, 유력자

moving average
이동 평균

muckraker
추문 폭로자, 부정부패
폭로자

multibuyer
다수구입자

multicasting *(computer)*
멀티케스팅

multicollinearity
다수 공직선성

multiemployer
다고용주

multiemployer bargaining
통일 단체 교섭

multifunction *(computer)*
다중기능

multimedia
멀티미디어

multinational corporation
 (MNC)
다국적 기업

multiple
자수의, 다량의

multiple listing
복합 열거

multiple locations forms
복수 소재지 서식

multiple regression
다줄회기

multiple retirement
 ages
복합 퇴직 연령

multiple shop
연쇄점

multiple-management
 plan
다각 경영 계획

multiple-peril insurance
복합위험보험

multiplier
승수

multiuser *(computer)*
다중 사용자

municipal bond
지방채

municipal revenue bond
지방 특정 재원 채권

muniments of title
부동산 권리증서

mutual association
상호협회

mutual company
상호회사

mutual fund
투자 신탁

mutual insurance
 company
상호보험 회사

mutuality of contract
계약의 상호성

N

naked option
무소유 주식 옵션
naked position
무소유 주식 옵션 상태
name position bond
기명식 지위신원
신용채권
name schedule bond
기명식 명세서부
신용채권
named peril policy
특정 위험보험
national wealth
국부
nationalization
국유화, 국영
natural business year
자연 회계연도
natural monopoly
자연 독점
natural resources
천연자원
navigation
항해
navigation (computer)
탐색
near money
준화폐

need satisfaction
수요 충족
negative
  amortization
마이너스 상각
negative carry
역이자 보유 (금융비용
이자가 채권 산출
이자보다 높음)
negative cash flow
현금 유출
negative correlation
역상관
negative income tax
역소득세
negative working
  capital
마이너스 운전자금
negligence
과실, 부주의
negociated price
할인가격
negotiable
교섭할 수 있는, 유통성이
있는, 양도 가능한
negotiable certificate of
  deposit
양도 가능 정기예금증서

negotiable instrument
유통증권

negotiable order of
  withdrawal (NOW)
양도가능 인출증서

negotiated market
  price
협정 시장 가격

negotiation
교부, 유통

neighborhood
  store
인근 가게

neoclassical economics
신고전파 경제학

nepotism
족벌주의, 친족 등용

nest egg
본전, 자금의 밑천

net
순, 최종의

net asset value (NAV)
순자산 가치

net assets
순자산, 순재산

net book value
순 장부가액

net contribution
순 부담금

net cost
순비용, 순원가

net current assets
순 유동자산, 운전자금

net income
순이익, 순익

net income per share of
  common stock
보통주 일주당 순익

net leasable area
순 임대차 가능지역

net lease
순임대 (임차인이 경비를
부담하는 임대차 계약)

net listing
수취액 지정 중개 (중개인
소개비는 판매가격에서
수취액을 뺀 금액)

net loss
순손실, 당기 순손실

net national product
국민 순생산

net operating income
  (NOI)
영업 순이익

net operating loss (NOL)
영업 순손실

net present value
  (NPV)
순 현재가치

net proceeds
순 매상고, 순 수취금

net profit
순이익, 당기 순이익

net profit margin
순 이윤폭, 순 이윤차액

net purchases
당기 순 매입액
net quick assets
순 당좌자산,
순 유동자산
net rate
순 비율
net realizable
 value
순 실현 가능액
net sales
순 매출액
net surfing *(computer)*
네트서핑
net transaction
순거래
(수수료 없는 거래)
net yield
순산출
network *(computer)*
네트워크
network administrator
 (computer)
네트워크 관리자
networking
개인적 정보망의 형성,
네트워킹
new issue
신주, 신규발행 채권
new money
뉴머니,
신규차입 자금

new town
신도시, 교외 주택지
newspaper syndicate
신문기사 배급조합
niche
틈새시장, 특정분야
night letter
야간 발송 전보
node *(computer)*
노드
no-growth
제로 성장
no-load fund
판매 수수료가 없는
펀드(기금)
nominal account
명목계정
nominal damages
명목적 손해배상
nominal interest rate
명목 이자율
nominal scale
명목상 차이,
근소한 차이
nominal wage
명목 임금
nominal yield
명목 수익율
nominee
명의인, 지명인, 임명인
noncallable
만기상환의

noncompetitive bid
비경쟁 입찰

nonconforming use
부적절 사용

**noncontestability
  clause**
불가쟁 조항

**noncumulative preferred
  stock**
비누적식 우선주

noncurrent asset
비유동자산,

고정자산

**nondeductibility of
  employer contributions**
비공제 고용자 분담금

**nondiscretionary
  trust**
한정 신탁

**nondisturbance
  clause**
권리 불침해 조항

nondurable goods
비내구재,

비내구 소비재

**nonformatted
  (computer)**
비포맷의

**nonglare
  (computer)**
방사 방지

nonmember bank
비회원 은행

nonmember firm
비회원 회사

nonmonetary item
비화폐성 항목

nonnegotiable instrument
유통 불능 증권

**nonoperating expense
  (revenue)**
영업외 비용 (수입)

nonparametric statistics
비파라미터적 통계,

비매개통계

nonperformance
불이행

nonproductive
비생산적

nonproductive loan
비생산적 융자

nonprofit accounting
비영리 회계

nonprofit corporation
비영리 기업

**nonpublic
  information**
비공개 정보

nonrecourse
상환청구 불능

nonrecurring charge
비경상적 비용,

임시손실

nonrefundable
상환 불능, 반제 불능

nonrefundable fee or
nonrefundable deposit
상환 불능 수수료 또는
상환 불능 예약금
nonrenewable natural
resources
재생불능의 천연자원
nonstock
corporation
비주식 법인
nonstore retailing
무점포 판매
nonvoting stock
무의결권 주식
no-par stock
무액면 주식
norm
표준, 책임 생산량
normal price
정상 가격
normal profit
정상 이익,
정상 이윤
normal retirement
age
정상 은퇴 연령
normal wear and
tear
통상의 마모
normative economics
규범경제학
no-strike clause
비동맹파업 조항

not for profit
비영리
not rated (NR)
평가하지 않은
notarize
(문서를) 공중해 받다,
인증하다
note
각서, 주석
note payable
지급할 어음, 어음 채무
note receivable
받을 어음
notebook computer
(computer)
노트북 컴퓨터
notice
공고, 공시, 통지, 신고
notice of cancellation
clause
해약 통지 조항
notice of default
채무 불이행 통지
notice to quit
해약 예고, 사직 권고
novation
개정, 계약의 경정,
갱신
NSF
자금 부족, 잔고 부족
nuisance
방해, 폐, 성가심

null and void

(법률상)

무효의

num lock key

(computer)

넘 록 키

O

objective
목적, 객관적인
objective value
객관적 가치
obligation bond
공채, 사채
obligee
채권자
obligor
채무자
observation test
입회 검사
obsolescence
진부화, 노후화
occupancy level
점유율, 이용율
occupancy, occupant
재산 점유, 사용 ; 점유자,
현재 거주자
occupation
직업, 업무
occupational
  analysis
직업 분석
occupational disease
직업병
occupational group
직업 집단

occupational hazard
직업상의 위험
odd lot
단주, 단물
odd page
  (computer)
홀수 페이지
odd-value pricing
단수가격 설정
off peak
피크를 지난, 한산한 때의
off the balance sheet
대차대조표외의
off the books
장부에 기장되지 않은
off time
한가한 때
offer
제공하다, 제의하다
offer and acceptance
제공과 인수,
매매 계약
offeree
수납자
offerer
제공자, 제의자
offering date
매출 기일

offering price
매출 가격, 제의가격

office management
사무 관리

official exchange rate
공정 교환 비율

off-line *(computer)*
오프라인

off-price
할인의

off-sale date
비 판매일

offset
상쇄하다, 오프셋 인쇄

offshore
해외에서, 국외에서, 앞바다의

off-site cost
부지 밖의 비용

oil and gas lease
채유권 리스

oligopoly
과점

ombudsman
옴부즈맨, 고충 처리원

omitted dividend
무배당

on account
신용계정, 정산 계정

on demand
주문용, 요구에 의한

on order
주문중의

on speculation (on spec)
투기적인

onboard computer *(computer)*
탑재 컴퓨터

one-cent sale
1 센트 세일

one-hundred-percent location
최고의 장소

one-minute manager
1 분 관리자

one-time buyer
한번 구입자

one-time rate
표준 매채 요금

on-line *(computer)*
온라인

on-line data base
온라인 데이터베이스

on-sale date
판매일

on-the-job training (OJT)
직장내 교육, 사내고육

open account
정산 계정, 실잔고 계정

open bid
공개 입찰

open dating
보존 최종기한 표시
open distribution
개방분배
open economy
개방경제
open house
주택개방, 일반 공개
open housing
주거 개방, 공정 주택 판매
정책
open interest
미결제 거래잔고
open listing
개방식 위임계약
open mortgage
총괄 저당권
open order
무조건 주문, 시가주문
open outcry
공개적 판매방식
open shop
오픈 샵
open space
오픈 스페이스, 공지, 광장
open stock
낱개로도 살 수 있는 세트
상품
open union
개방조합
open-door policy
문호개방정책

open-end
무제한의
open-end lease
개방형 리스
open-end management
  company
개방식 경영회사
open-end mortgage
개방형 담보
opening
개방, 공지, 개장
open-market rates
시중금리
open-to-buy
구매 여력, 발주 잔고
operand
피연산수
operating cycle
영업 주기, 거래 주기
operating expense
영업 비용, 운전 비용
operation mode
작동상태
operation mode
  (computer)
연산모드
operational audit
업무감사, 운영 감사
operational control
현장 통제
operations research
  OR)
경영 연구, 작전 연구

operator
(computer)
오퍼레이터
opinion
의견, 감사의견
opinion leader
여론 주도자
opinion of title
부동산 물건에 대한
변호사 의견서
opportunity cost
기회 원가, 기회 비용
optical character
recognition (OCR)
(computer)
광학식 문자 인식
optical fiber
(computer)
광섬유
optimum capacity
최적 조업도
option
옵션, 선택권, 주식 구입
선택권
option holder
옵션 보유자
optional modes of
settlement
(보험금) 지불선택조항
or better
(주식의) 지정가 이상
oral contract
구두 계약

orange goods
오렌지 상품
order
주문, 주문서, 명령, 순서
order bill of lading
양도성 선화증권
order card
작업 지시서
order entry
주문입력, 수주
order flow
pattern
주문 이동 패턴
order form
주문서, 주문 서식
order number
주문 번호
order paper
주문 서류
order regulation
주문의 규칙
order-point system
주문점 시스템
ordinal scale
순서 척도, 서열 척도
ordinance
법령, 포고, 조례, 정부
명령, 규정
ordinary and necessary
business expense
통상적으로 필요한
영업비

ordinary annuity
정상 연금, 보통연금
ordinary course of
business
보통의 업무과정
ordinary gain or ordinary
income
경상수입, 경상소득
ordinary interest
통상 금리
ordinary loss
경상 손실
ordinary payroll exclusion
endorsement
통상 봉급 제외 지시
organization
조직, 지구, 협회
organization cost
창업비
organization development
조직 개발
organization planning
조직 계획
organization structure
조직 구조
organizational behaviour
조직 행동
organizational chart
조직도, 회사 구성도
organized labor
조직 노동
orientation
적응 지도, 집무 예비교육

original cost
취득 원가
original entry
원초 기입
original issue discount
(OID)
발매시 할인
original maturity
발매와 만기사이
original order
최초의 주문
origination fee
융자개시 수수료
originator
창작자, 원래의 자산
소유자
other income
영업외 수익
other insurance clause
타보험 조항
other people's money
차입금
out of the money
상금이 없는
outbid
(경매에서) 고가를 부르다
outcry market
경매시장
outlet store
아웃렛 점, 직매점
outline view
윤곽도

outline view
  (computer)
아웃라인 뷰
outside director
사외이사, 사외중역
outsourcing
아웃소싱, 외부위탁
outstanding
미결제의, 미해결의, 눈에
띠는
outstanding balance
미불 잔고, 융자 잔고
outstanding capital stock
주식발행고
over (short)
이상
over the counter (OTC)
장외 거래의
overage
규정 연령을 초과한, 과잉
공급
overall expenses
  method
총비용 방식
overall rate of return
총수익률
over-and-short
과부족의
overbooked
초과 예약 상태인
overbought
과매수

overcharge
부당한 가격 요구
overflow
과당, 과잉
overhang
돌출한, 잉여의
overhead
간접비
overheating
(경기의) 과열
overimprovement
과잉 개량
overissue
(지폐, 등권을) 남발하다
overkill
지나침, 과잉
overpayment
지불 초과
overproduction
과잉생산
override
번복하다,
무효로하다
overrun
초과
over-the-counter
retailing
장외거래 소매
overtime
잔업 시간, 초과 근무시간
overtrading
자금 초과거래, 과다거래

overvalued
과대평가의
overwrite
 (computer)
겹쳐쓰기

owner-operator
자영업자
ownership
소유권
ownership form
소유 형태

P

p value
P 가치

pacesetter
진도 설정자

package
패키지, 소포, 일괄 거래

package band
(광고나 특별 가격이 있는)
포장 띠

package code
패키지 코드,
패키지 부호

package design
포장 디자인

package mortgage
일괄 저당

packaged goods
포장된 상품

packing list
포장 명세서

padding
부정의 경비 추가

page break *(computer)*
페이지 분리

page down *(computer)*
페이지 다운

page format *(computer)*
페이지 포맷

page up *(computer)*
페이지 업

pagination *(computer)*
페이지 매김

paid in advance
선불

paid status
지불 상태

paid-in capital
불입 자금

paid-in surplus
불입 잉여금

Paintbrush
  (computer)
페인트 브러시

painting the tape
증권 위장 인수와 판매

palmtop
  (computer)
팜탑 컴퓨터

paper
지폐, 서류

paper gold
IMF 의 특별인출권

paper jam
  (computer)
종이 걸림

paper money
지폐

paper profit (loss)
가공이익 (손실)
par
액면가격
par bond
액면가격 채권
par value
액면가액
paralegal
변호사 (법률가)
보조원(의)
parallel connection
(computer)
병렬 연결
parallel processing
병렬 처리
parameter
매개변수
parcel
한 필지, 소포
parent company
모회사
parity
패리티, 동등, 평형 가격
parity check
패리티 검사,
홀수짝수 검사
parity price
패리티 가격, 평형 가격
parking
(재산, 돈의) 임시 거치,
주차장

parliament procedure
의사진행 절차
partial delivery
분할 배달
partial release
저당 일부 해제, 단계적
해제
partial taking
토지의 일부 수용
partial-equilibrium
analysis
부분균형 분석
participating insurance
이익배당 보험
participating policy
이익배당 보험증서
participating preferred
stock
참가 우선주
participation certificate
참가 증서
participation loan
협조 융자
participative budgeting
참여 예산
participative leadership
참여 지도자
partition
구획, 구분
partner
파트너, 조합원, 공동
경영자, 사원

partnership
공동 협력
part-time
파트타임, 비상근
passed dividend
미불 배당
passenger mile
여객 마일
passive activities
수동적 활동
passive income
 (loss)
소극적 소득(손실)
passive investor
소극적 투자가
passport
여권
pass-through security
패스드루 증권,
투자가에게 수입이
전달되는 증권
password
 (computer)
패스워드, 암호
past service benefit
과거근무 연금(혜택)
paste (computer)
붙이다
patent
특허권
patent infringement
특허권 침해

patent monopoly
특허권 독점, 전매 특허
patent of invention
발명 특허
patent pending
특허 출원중
patent warfare
특허 전쟁
paternalism
부권주의, 부권적 간섭
path (computer)
패스
patronage dividend and
 rebate
장려 이익 배당과 할인
pauper
극빈자, 빈민
pay
지급, 급여,
지불
pay as you go
현금 지급방식
pay period
지불 기간
payables
지급 채무
payback period
회수 기간
paycheck
급여수표
payday
급여일

payee
수취인
payer
지급인
paying agent
지불 대리인
payload
유료 하중
payment bond
지불보증, 반환 보증 채권
payment date
지불일
payment in due course
만기지불
payment method
지불 방법
payola
사례, 뇌물
payout
지불금, 배당금, 원금 회수
payout ratio
배당 비율
payroll
임금, 급료
payroll deduction
임금공제
payroll savings plan
급료 예금 계획
payroll tax
급여세금
peak
(경기의) 최고점

peak period
성수기
peculation
공금횡령
pecuniary
금전 상위, 재정적
peg
가격 지지
penalty
형벌, 벌금,
위약금
penny stock
투기적 저가격 주식
pension fund
연금 기금
peon
일용 근로자,
날품팔이
people intensive
사람 집약적
per capita
일인당
per diem
1 일 단위, 일당,
하루 사용료
per-capita debt
일인당 부채
percent,
  percentage
백분율
percentage lease
보합제 임대차율

percentage-of-completion
method
공사 진행 비율법

percentage-of-sales
method
매상 비율법

percolation test
침투 시험

perfect (pure)
monopoly
완전 독점

perfect competition
완전 경쟁

perfected
완벽하게 한(된)

performance
이행, 업적, 성능, 효율

performance bond
계약 이행 보증, 계약 보증
보험

performance fund
퍼포먼스 펀드, 적극형
펀드

performance stock
업적주

period
기간, 사업연도, 회계 기간

period expense, period
cost
기간 비용, 기간 원가

periodic inventory
method
정기적 재고 조사법

peripheral device
(computer)
주변 기기

perishable
썩기쉬운 (물건)

perjury
위증죄

permanent difference
영구적 차이

permanent financing
영구적 자금 조달

permit
허가, 허가증

permit bond
허가 보증

permutations
순열, 치환

perpetual inventory
계속기록법

perpetuity
영구연금, 종신연금

perquisite (perk)
부수입

person
사람, 당사자, 거래 관계자

personal data sheet
개인 자료표

personal digital assistant
(PDA) (computer)
개인 휴대정보 단말기

personal financial
statement
개인의 재산상황 보고서

personal holding company
 (PHC)
개인 지주 회사
personal income
개인 소득
personal influence
개인적 영향
personal injury
인신 상해
personal liability
개인적 책임,
개인적 부채
personal property
동산, 개인 재산
personal property
 floater
동산 포괄보험
personal selling
대개인 판매,
인적 판매
personnel
직원, 인원, 인재
personnel department
인사과, 인사 부문
petition
청원, 청원서, 진정서
petty cash fund
소액 현금
Phillips' curve
필립스 곡선
physical commodity
유형의 상품

physical depreciation
물리적 감가, 물량적 감가
physical examination
신체검사, 건강 진단
physical inventory
실지 재고, 현 재고량
picketing
피케팅(요구, 불만을
호소하는 시위)
picture format *(computer)*
픽처 포맷
pie chart/graph
(computer)
파이 차트/그래프
piece rate
성과급, 단가
piece work
삯일, 청부 업무
pier to house
화물 인수자에게 화물이
직접 배달됨
piggyback loan
피기백 론, 두 사람이
대부받는 저당
pilot plan
실험적 계획
pin money
용돈, 소액의 돈
pipeline
유통 경로, 수송관, 보급선
pitch *(computer)*
피치

pixel image *(computer)*
픽셀 이미지

pixel/picture element
픽셀/픽처 요소

place utility
장소 효과

placement test
배치 시험

plain text
보통 본문

plain text *(computer)*
일반 텍스트

plaintiff
소송인, 원고, 고소인

plan
계획

plan B
계획 B, 제 2 안

planned economy
계획적 경제

plant
공장, 시설

plat
도면, 작은 땅

plat book
토지 등록부

pleading
변론, 고소장, 소송절차

pledge
언약, 보증, 저당

plot
음모, 구상, 계획

plot plan
배치도, 부지 계획도

plottage value
부지 가치

plotter
음모자, 지도 제작자, 플로터

plow back
(이익의) 재투자

plus tick
경기의 상승

pocket computer
 (computer)
포켓 컴퓨터

point
포인트 (채권가격의 퍼센트 변화)

point chart *(computer)*
점지도

poison pill
기업 매수에 대한 금융 방어책

poisson distribution
포이송 분포

police power
경찰권, 치안 유지권

policy holder
보험 계약자

policy loan
보험증권 대부

pollution
오염

pool
기업 연합, 공공 출자
pooling of interests
지분 풀링
portal-to-portal
 pay
근무시간제 임금
portfolio
포트폴리오, 유가증권
명세서
portfolio beta score
포트폴리오 가격 변동
비교
portfolio income
포트폴리오 소득
portfolio insurance
포트폴리오 재보험
portfolio manager
직업적인 포트폴리오
관리자
portrait (format)
 (computer)
세로 방향, 포트레이트
position
위치
positioning
포지셔닝
positive confirmation
적극적 확인
positive leverage
차입 자본을 이용하여
투자 이익을 올림

positive yield curve
장기채권의 이율이
단기채권보다 높음
possession
소유, 점유, 소유물
post closing trial
 balance
결산후 시산표
posting (computer)
포스팅, 투고 메시지
poverty
빈곤
power connection
 (computer)
전원 접속
power down
 (computer)
전원을 끄다
power of attorney
위임장, 위임권, 대리권
power of sale
매각권
power surge
전류, 전압의 급증
power up
 (computer)
전원을 켜다
practical capacity
실제 생산 능력
pre-bill
예비청구
precautionary motive
경계적 동기

preclosing
복잡한 결산 예행 연습

precompute
분할 불입에서 이자를
미리 계산함

prediction
예측

preemptive rights
신주 인수권

preexisting use
(토지의) 선재 사용

prefabricated
사전에 만들어진, 조립식

preferential rehiring
우선적 재고용

preferred dividend
우선주 배당

preferred dividend
coverage
우선배당 적용율

preferred stock
우선주

preliminary
 prospectus
예비 계획서, 임시 계획서

premises
구내, 건물이 딸린 토지

premium
보험금, 액면 초과액,
할증금

premium bond
할증금이 붙은 채권

premium income
보험료 수입

premium pay
장려금 지불

premium rate
할증요금, 특별요금,
보험료율

prenuptial agreement
결혼전의 동의 계약

prepaid
선불한

prepaid expense
선급 비용

prepaid interest
선급 이자

prepayment
선급금, 전도금, 선불

prepayment clause
선불 조항

prepayment penalty
선납 벌칙금

prepayment
 privilege
선납 특권

prerelease
건축전 리스 계약

prerogative
특권, 특전

presale
세일전 특별 세일

prescription
명령, 처방, 시효

present fairly
공평한 제시
present value
현재 가치, 현재 가격
present value of 1
1 의 현재가격
present value of annuity
연금의 현재가격
presentation
제출, 제시
president
대통령, 사장
presold issue
사전 매각된 공채 발행
press kit
기자 회견 자료
prestige advertising
위신 광고, 프레스티지
광고
prestige pricing
명성의 가격
pretax earnings
과세전 수입
pretax rate of return
과세전 수익율
preventive
 maintenance
예방 정비
price elasticity
가격 탄력성
price index
가격지수

price lining
가격 라이닝, 제한된 수의
가격 사용
price stabilization
가격 안정
price support
가격 유지
price system
가격 제도, 가격 체제
price war
가격 전쟁
price-fixing
가격 설정, 가격 조작
pricey
비싼, 고가의
pricing below market
시장 가격 이하의 가격 매김
primary boycott
1 차적 보이콧
primary demand
기본적 수요, 1 차적 수요
primary distribution
제 1 차 매출, 제 1 차 분배
primary earnings per
 (common) share
기본적 1 (보통)
주당 이익
primary lease
제 1 차 임차권
primary market
발행 시장, 일차 시장,
주요 시장

primary market
 area
주요 시장 지역
primary package
상품의 주된 포장
prime paper
우량 기업 어음
prime rate
최저 대출 금리
prime tenant
주요 차용자
principal
원금, 중요한
principal amount
원금
principal and interest
 payment (P&I)
원금과 이자 지불
principal residence
주 주거지, 주소
principal stock holder
주요 주주
principal sum
(지불되는 보험금의)
최고액, 원금
principal, interest, taxes
 and insurance payment
 (PITI)
원금, 이자, 세금과 보험
지불금
printer
 (computer)
프린터

printout
 (computer)
출력 정보
prior period adjustment
전기의 손익 수정
prior service cost
이전의 용역 비용
prior-preferred stock
이전의 우선주
privacy laws
사생활 권리법
private cost
사적 비용
private limited ownership
사적 제한된 소유
private mortgage
 insurance
민간 저당 보험
private offering or private
 placement
개별 모집
privatization
민영화
privity
당사자간의 관계
prize broker
일류 브로커
probate
(유언의) 검인, 입증
probationary employee
견습 종업원, 가채용 종업원
proceeds
수입, 매상고, 매상금

proceeds from resale
재판매 수입, 재판매의
매상고

processor upgrade
  (computer)
처리기 업그레이드,
프로세서 업그레이드

procurement
조달, 획득

procuring cause
구매 이유

produce
생산하다, 제조하다

producer cooperative
생산자 협동조합

producer goods
생산재

product
제품

product liability
제품 책임, 제조물 책임

product liability
  insurance
제품 책임보험

product life cycle
제품 생애 주기

product line
제품 계열

product mix
제품 배합

production
생산, 제조

production control
생산 관리

production rate
생산율

production worker
생산 노동자

production-oriented
  organization
생산지향 조직

production-possibility
  curve
생산가능성 곡선

productivity
생산성, 생산력

profession
직업, 전문직

profit
이익, 이윤

profit and commissions
form
이익과 수수료 양식

profit and loss statement
  (P&L)
손익계산서

profit center
이익 책임 단위,
이익 중심점

profit margin
매출액 이익율

profit motive
영리주의, 이윤 동기

profit squeeze
이익 압박

profit system
이윤 제도

profit taking
이윤 획득

profitability
수익성, 이익율

profiteer
부당 이득자, 폭리 상인

profit-sharing
 plan
이익배분 제도

program budgeting
프로그램 예산

program trade
프로그램 매매

programmer
프로그래머

programming language
 (computer)
프로그래밍 언어

progress payments
분할 지급, 분납

progressive tax
누진 과세

projected (pro forma)
 financial statement
추정 재무제표

projected benefit
 obligation
예측 연금채무, 추정
급부채무

projection
계획, 견적, 예상

promissory note
약속어음

promotion mix
판매 촉진 혼합 방법

promotional
 allowance
판매 촉진 할인

proof of loss
손실 증명

property
재산, 부동산, 소유권,
특성

property line
토지의 경계선

property management
재산 관리, 부동산 관리

property report
재산 보고

property rights
재산권

property tax
재산세

proprietary interest
소유권, 지분

proprietary lease
소유자 임대계약

proprietorship
개인기업

prorate
할당하다, 비례 배분하다

prospect
견적액, 예측, 장래성

prospective rating
예상 요율산정
prospectus
취지서, 발기서, 목록
색인, 사업 설명서
protected file
(computer)
보호된 파일
protectionism
보호주의
protocol
원안, 조약안, 의정서,
규약
proviso
단서, 조건
proxy
대리인, 투표권의 위임
proxy right
대리권
proxy statement
주주에게 보내는
연차보고서
prudence
신중, 조심, 검약
psychic income
심리적 수입
public accounting
공공 회계
public domain
공유
public employee
공무원

public file (computer)
공공 파일
public record
공문서
public relations
 (PR)
홍보, 공보, 선전 활동
public sale
공개 매각
public use
공용
public works
공공 사업
publicly held
공공 소유의
puffing
재산 부풀리기
pull-down menu
 (computer)
풀다운 메뉴
pump priming
(정부의) 경기 진흥책
punch list
미결제 사항의 표
punitive damages
징벌적 손해 배상
purchase
매입, 구매, 매수
purchase journal
매입 분개장
purchase money
 mortgage
구입 대금 저당

purchase order
매입 주문서
purchasing power
구매력
pure capitalism
순수 자본주의
pure competition
순수 경쟁
pure-market economy
순수 시장 경제
purge *(computer)*
지우다, 제거하다

push money
 (PM)
특별 장려금
put option
매각 선택권
put to seller
매각
선택권 실행
pyramiding
피라미딩,
계속 이익을 보는 증권

Q

qualified endorsement
무담보 배서,

한정 배서

qualified opinion
한정 의견 감사 보고서

qualified plan or qualified trust
수급 자격 제도(신탁)

qualified terminable interest property (Q-TIP) trust
수급 자격 기한부 이자

재산 신탁

qualitative analysis
정성 분석

qualitative research
정성 조사

quality
품질, 특성

quality control
품질 관리

quality engineering
품질 공학

quantitative analysis
정량 분석

quantitative research
정량 조사

quantity discount
수량 할인

quarterly
분기별

quasi contract
준계약

query *(computer)*
질문

queue *(computer)*
큐

quick asset
당좌자산, 유동자산

quick ratio
당좌비율

quiet enjoyment
평온 향유권

quiet title suit
토지소유권 보전 소송

quitclaim deed
권리 포기형 양도증서

quo warranto
심문 영장

quorum
정족수, 선발자 집단

quota
할당, 분담

quota sample
할당 표본

quotation
시가, 시세

qwerty keyboard
  (computer)
쿼티 키보드

qwertz keyboard
  (computer)
쿼츠 키보드

R

racket
부정한 돈벌이, 밀매
rag content
(종이의) 섬유 함유량
raider
(시장) 교란자, 침입자
rain insurance
강우 보험
raised check
위조 방지 수표
rally
(경기가) 회복되다
random access memory (RAM) *(computer)*
랜덤 액세스 메모리
random sample
무작위 추출 견본
random walk
난보
random-digit dialing
무작위 추출 다이얼링
random-number generator
난수 발생기
range *(computer)*
범위, 한계
rank and file
평사원, 대중, 일반인

ratable
평가할 수 있는, 과세해야 할
rate
비율, 요금, 임금, 세금
rate base
요금 산정 기준,(잡지의 보증 부수)
rate card
요금표
rate setting
요율 설정
rated policy
요율 보험 증권
rates and classifications
요율과 등급
ratification
추인, 비준, 승인
rating
등급, 보험 요율 산정, 신용도 평가
ratio analysis
경영분석, 비율 분석
ratio scale
비례 척도
rationing
배급

raw data
원시 데이터

raw land
미개발지

raw material
원료, 재료

reading the
  tape
주식 가격 모니터

readjustment
재조정

read-only (computer)
읽기 전용의

real
진짜의, 실재하는

real account
실질 계정

real earnings
실질 소득

real estate
부동산

real estate investment
  trust (REIT)
부동산 투자 신탁

real estate market
부동산 시장

real estate owned
  (REO)
부동산 소유자

real income
실질 소득

real interest rate
실질 이자율

real property
부동산

real rate of return
실질 이익율

real value of money
화폐의 실질가치

real wages
실질 임금

realized gain
실현 이익

realtor
부동산업자

reappraisal lease
재평가 리스

reasonable person
사리를 아는 사람

reassessment
재평가

rebate
할인, 리베이트

reboot (computer)
리부트

recall (computer)
회수, 리콜

recall campaign
리콜 캠페인

recall study
리콜 연구,
회수 연구

recapitalization
자본 구성의 변경, 자본
수정

recapture
회수

recapture rate
회수율

recasting a debt
부채를 다시 계산하다

receipt, receipt
 book
영수증, 영수대장

receivables turnover
매출 채권 회전율

receiver
수취인, 재산 관리인

receiver's certificate
재산 관리인 증명서

receivership
관재인의 직무, 재산 관리
상태

receiving clerk
수입계, 수취계

receiving record
영수기록, 수취 기록

recession
불경기, 경기 후퇴

reciprocal buying
상호 구매

reciprocity
상호 주의, 상호 이익

reckoning
계산, 집계

recognition
인식

recognized gain
인식 이익

recompense
배상, 보상

reconciliation
조정, 화해

reconditioning property
재산의 수리

reconsign
재위탁하다, 재위임하다

reconveyance
재양도, 전 소유권자에
반환

record
기록, 장부, 레코드

recorder point
레코드 포인트

recording
리코딩, 기록

records management
기록 정보 관리

recoup, recoupment
되찾다, 회복하다, 공제,
배상

recourse
상환 청구, 상환, 추심

recourse loan
상환 준비 대부

recover (computer)
재생시키다

recovery
회복

recovery fund
회복 자금

recovery of basis
기준의 회복

recruitment
채용, 모집, 보충

recruitment bonus
채용 상여금

recycle bin *(computer)*
휴지통

recycling
재생(이용)

red tape
관료적 형식주의

redeem
변제하다, 상환하다

redemption
상환

redemption period
상환 기간

redevelop
재개발하다

rediscount
재할인, 재할인하다

rediscount rate
재할인율

redlining
특정 경계 지역 지정

reduced rate
할인 요금

reduction certificate
할인 보증서

referee
심판원, 중재인

referral
참조, 조회

refinance
재금융, 리파이낸스

reformation
재구성, 개량

refresh *(computer)*
재생하다, 리프레시하다

refund
상환하다, 반환하다,
상환금, 반환금

refunding
반제 상환

registered bond
기명식 채권, 등록식 채권

registered check
등록식 수표

registered company
등록된 회사

registered investment
  company
등록된 투자회사

registered representative
등록 대리인

registered security
기명 증권

registrar
등기계, 등록계, 주주명부

registration
등록

registration statement
등록 신고서
registry of deeds
날인 증서의 등록
regression analysis
희귀분석법
regression line
희귀선
regressive tax
역진세
regular-way delivery
  (and settlement)
통상 방법의 배달
(과 결제)
regulated
  commodities
통제 상품,
규제 상품
regulated industry
통제 산업,
규제 산업
regulated investment
  company
규제 투자 회사
regulation
규칙, 규제, 조정
regulatory agency
통제 기관, 규제 기관
rehabilitation
재생, 재건, 부흥
reindustrialization
재공업화

reinstatement
복권, 회복, 계약 부활
reinsurance
재보험
reinvestment privilege
재투자 특권
reinvestment rate
재투자 수익율
related party
  transaction
특수 관계자간 거래
release
면제, 권리 포기
release clause
면제 조항,해제 조항
relevance
목적 적합성
reliability
신뢰성, 신뢰도
relocate
재배치하다
remainder
잉여, 잔여권
remainderman
잔여권자
remedy
구제
remit
지불하다, 면제하다
경감하다
remit rate
지불 비율

remonetization
재통화제정

**remote access
 (computer)**
원격 접근

remuneration
보수, 보상, 급료

renegociate
재교섭하다

**renegotiated rate
 mortgage (RRM)**
재조정 금리 저당

**renewable natural
 resource**
재생가능 천원자원

renewal option
갱신 선택권

rent
임대료, 임대차

rent control
임대료 통제

rentable area
임대가능 면적

rental rate
임대료

rent-free period
무료 임대 기간

reopener clause
교섭 재개 조항

reorganization
재조직, 재편성

repairs
수선 작업

repatriation
(이익금) 송환

replace
바꾸다, 대체하다

**replace
 (computer)**
바꾸다, 대체하다

replacement cost
대체 원가, 재조달 원가

**replacement cost
 accounting**
대체 원가 회계

replacement reserve
설비 갱신 준비금

replevin
동산 점유권 회복

reporting currency
재무 보고 통화

repressive tax
억제적 과세

reproduction cost
재생산 비용

repudiation
거절, 부인

**repurchase agreement
 (REPO; RP)**
환매조건부 채권
매매계약

reputation
평판, 명성

**request for proposal
 (RFP)**
제안 요구서

required rate of return	residential
요구 이익율	주택의, 주거의
requisition	residential broker
청구, 요청	주택 중개업자
resale proceeds	residential district
전소유주가 판매후	주택 지역
실제받는 금액	residential energy credit
rescission	주택 에너지 융자
계약 해제	residential service
research	contract
연구, 조사	주택 서비스 계약
research and development	residual value
(R&D)	잔존 가액, 잔존 가치
연구 개발	resolution
research department	결의
연구 부서	resource
research intensive	자원
연구 집약적	respondent
reserve	응하는, 피고의 입장에
적립금, 충당금	있는
reserve fund	response
준비자금, 적립금	응답
reserve requirement	response projection
준비자금 규정	응답의 예측
reserve-stock control	restart (computer)
예약 주식 통제	다시 시작하다
reset (computer)	restitution
재기동하다, 리셋하다	반환, 원상 회복
resident buyer	restraint of trade
주재 구매자	거래 제한
resident buying office	restraint on alienation
주재 구매 사무소	양도 제한

restricted surplus
제한된 잉여금

restriction
규제, 제한, 한정

restrictive covenant
(토지 사용의)

제한 계약

retail
소매

retail credit
소매 신용

retail display
  allowance
소매 진열 할인

retail inventory
  method
소매 재고법

retail outlet
소매 판매점

retail rate
소매 가격(비율)

retailer's service
  program
소매상의 매상 증진
프로그램

retained earnings
이익 적립금

retained earnings
  statement
보유 이익 계산서

retained earnings,
  appropriated
특별 보유 이익

retaining
보유

retaliatory eviction
보복적 추출

retire
퇴직하다, 은퇴하다

retirement
은퇴, 퇴직, 회수

retirement age
정년, 퇴직 연령

retirement fund
은퇴 기금

retirement income
은퇴 소득

retirement plan
퇴직금 제도

retroactive
소급적하는, 소급적인

retroactive adjustment
소급 조정

return
신고서, 이익

return of capital
투자의 회수,

자본의 회수

return on equity
주식자본 이익

return on invested capital
투자자본 이익

return on pension plan
  assets
연금계획자산 이익

return on sales
매출액 이익율

returns
이윤, 보고, 반환

revaluation
재평가

revenue
수익, 매상, 세입

revenue anticipation note (RAN)
수입 예상 증권

revenue bond
수익 담보 채권, 특정재원 채권

revenue ruling
내국 세입 규칙

reversal
반전, 전환

reverse annuity mortgage (RAM)
역주택담보 대출

reverse leverage
역차입 자본 이용 효과

reverse split
역분활, 주식 병합

reversing entry
역분개, 재정리 분개

reversion
복구 가치, 회복권

reversionary factor
복귀 요인

reversionary interest
(재산의) 복귀 권리

reversionary value
복귀 가치

review
검토, 재조사

revocable trust
철회 가능한 신탁

revocation
철회, 폐지, 취소

revolving charge account
회전 외상 매출 계정

revolving credit
회전 신용 계정

revolving fund
회전 자금

rezoning
재구분, 구분 변경

rich
부유한, 풍부한

rich text format (RTF) (computer)
RFT, 리치 텍스트 포멧

rider
추서, 첨부 서류, 추가 조항

right of first refusal
최우선 인수권 행사의 거절

right of redemption
회수권

right of rescission
해약권, 철회권

right of return
반환권

right of survivorship
생존자 재산권

right-of-way
우선 통행권, 통행권

risk
위험, 위험 부담

risk arbitrage
위헌을 수반한 재정거래

risk averse
위험을 회피하는

risk management
위기관리

risk-adjusted discount rate
위험 조정 할인율

rolling stock
(철도의) 차량

rollover
롤오버

rollover loan
롤오버 대출

ROM (read-only memory) *(computer)*
롬, 읽기용 기억장치

rotating shift
교대제, 윤번

round lot
거래 단위

roundhouse
원형 기관차고

royalty
특허권 사용료

royalty trust
특허권 사용료 신탁

run
경영하다, 계속하다

run of paper (ROP)
게재 위치를 편집자에게 일임하는 광고

run with the land
토지 사용권이나 제한의 이전

rundown
황폐한, 감원

rural
시골의, 전원의

rurban
전원 도시, 교외에 있는

S

sabotage
사보타주, 파괴 행위, 방해
행위
safe harbor rule
안전항 규정, (세금의)
승인 영역 규정
safekeeping
보관, 보호, 보전
safety commission
안전 수수료
safety margin
안전한 범위의 영업 이익
salariat
봉급생활자 계층
salary
급료, 봉급
salary reduction
plan
봉급 감소 계획
sale
판매, 매출
sale and
leaseback
매각후 임차, 판매후 리스
sale or exchange
매출 또는 교환
sales analyst
판매 분석가

sales budget
판매 예산, 매출 예산
sales charge
판매 비용
sales contract
판매 계약
sales effectiveness test
판매 효과 시험
sales incentive
판매 장려 수당
sales journal
매출 분개장
sales letter
세일즈 레터(편지)
sales portfolio
세일즈 포트폴리오,
세일즈 자료
sales promotion
판매 촉진, 판촉 활동
sales returns and
allowances
반품 조정과 예비비
sales revenue
매출액
sales tax
판매세
sales type lease
판매형 리스

salesperson
판매원, 점원

salvage value
잔존가(액)

sample buyer
견본 구입자

sampling
표본 추출법

sandwich lease
샌드위치 리스, 전대

satellite communication
위성 통신

satisfaction of a debt
부채의 상환

satisfaction piece
채무이행 증서,

변제증서

savings bond
저축성 채권

savings element
(생명보험의) 저축 요소

savings rate
저축률

scab
비조합원, 노동조합

불참가자

scalage
공제율

scale *(computer)*
크기 조정

scale order
스케일 구매

scale relationship
비례 관계

scalper
단기 투자의 시세 차익을

챙기는 사람

scanner *(computer)*
스캐너

scarcity, scarcity value
품기, 휘귀 가치

scatter diagram
산포 도표

scatter plan
산포 도면

scenic easement
경관 지역권

schedule
예정표, 계획하다

scheduled production
계획생산

scheduling
스케줄링

scienter
도의로, 의도적으로, 고의

scope of employment
고용 범위

scorched-earth defense
초토화 방어

screen filter
 (computer)
스크린 필터

screen saver *(computer)*
화면 보호기

scrip
단수증권, 증서,
서류
scroll down
 (computer)
스크롤 다운
scroll up (computer)
스크롤 업
seal
인장, 증인, 실인
seal of approval
확인의 인장
sealed bid
봉함 입찰
search engine
 (computer)
검색 엔진
seasonal adjustment
계절 조정
seasonality
계절성
seasoned issue
확실한 증권
seasoned loan
견실한 융자
seat
회원권
second lien or second
 mortgage
제 2 순위 저당, 2 번 저당
second mortgage
 lending
제 2 순위 저당 대부

secondary boycott
제 2 차 보이콧, 제 2 차
불매운동
secondary distribution
제 2 차 판매, 기관판매
secondary market
유통시장, 제 2 차 시장
secondary mortgage
 market
제 2 차 저당시장
second-preferred
 stock
저순위 우선주
sector
부분, 분야, 영역
secured bond
담보부 사채
secured debt
담보부 부채
secured transaction
담보부 거래
securities
증권, 유가 증권
securities analyst
증권 분석가
securities and
 commodities exchanges
증권상품거래소
Securities and Exchange
 Commission (SEC)
미국 증권거래 위원회
securities loan
증권담보 대출

security
보증, 담보, 저당

security deposit
보증금

security interest
약정 담보권, 유가증권
이자

security rating
담보 평가

seed money
착수 자금

segment margin
사업 부문별 마진

segment reporting
부문별 보고서

segmentation strategy
부문화 전략

segregation of duties
업무 분장

seisin
(토지의) 소유권

select
선택하다, 선택

select (computer)
선택하다, 선택

selective credit control
선택적 신용 통제

selective distribution
선택적 판매, 선택적 판매
경로

self employed
자영업의, 자영업자의

self insurance
자가 담보

self-amortizing mortgage
자기 상환적 저당대부

self-directed ira
자기 결정의 개인 퇴직
적립 계정

self-help
자조, 자조 노력

self-tender offer
자사 주식의 공개 매입

seller's market
판매자 시장

sell-in
에서 팔다

selling agent or selling
  broker
판매 대리점 또는 판매
중개인

selling climax
대량 매물로 인한 주가의
대폭락

selling short
공매하다

sell-off
대량 매물로 인한 대폭락

semiannual
반년 마다의

semiconductor
반도체

semimonthly
월 2 회

semivariable costs
반변동 비용

senior debt
우위변제 채무, 상위채무

senior refunding
우선 상환

senior security
우선 담보

sensitive market
불안정 시장

sensitivity training
집단 감수성 훈련

sentiment indicators
경향 지시기

separate property
특유재산

serial bond
연속상환 채권

serial port (computer)
시리얼 포트

series bond
연속 발행 채권

server (computer)
서버

service
용역, 업무

service bureau
서비스 기관

service club
봉사 클럽

service department
서비스 부문

service economy
서비스 경제

service fee
봉사료

service worker
근무자

servicing
공급

setback
좌절, 퇴보

setoff
상쇄

settle
청산하다, 결산하다

settlement
결제, 변제, 청산

settlement date
결제일

settlor
재산 양도자,
설정자

severalty
(재산의) 단독 보유

severance damages
(토지의) 분할 피해

severance pay
퇴직금,
해고 수당

sexual harassment
성희롱

shakedown
강탈, 갈취

shakeout
도태, 쇄신, 소투자가의
도태
shakeup
(조직의) 대정리, 재편성
share
몫, 공유, 주식
sharecropper
물납 소작인
shared drive *(computer)*
공유 드라이브
shared-appreciation
 mortgage (SAM)
저당 물건 증가분 공유
조건 대부
shared-equity mortgage
저당 물건 공유 조건 대부
shareholder
주주
shareholder's equity
자기 자본
shares authorized
수권 주식
shareware *(computer)*
셰어웨어 (저작권이 있는
소프트웨어, 일정 기간
시험 사용 후 계속해서
사용하고 싶을 때에
요금을 지불하는 것)
shark repellent
기업 매수 방지책

shark watcher
기업 매수 대응 감시
전문가
sheet feeder
 (computer)
시트 피더
shell corporation
유령회사, 가공회사
shift
변동, 교대
shift differential
교대 근무 수당
shift key *(computer)*
시프트 키
shift lock *(computer)*
시프트 록
shop
상점, 공장, 근무처
shopper
물건 사는 사람
shopping service
쇼핑 서비스
short bond
단기채권, 단기사채
short covering
숏 커버링, 환매
short form
간이형
short interest
공매 총액
short position
공매자의 입장

short squeeze
매도 스퀴즈
short term
단기
shortfall
부족, 부족분
short-sale rule
공매 규정
short-term capital gain (loss)
단기간의 자본이득 (손해)
short-term debt or short-term liability
단기 채무,
단기 차입금
shrinkage
축소, 감소
shut down (computer)
셧다운
shutdown
폐쇄, 영업 정지
sight draft
일람지불 어음
sign off (computer)
종료 신호
sign on (computer)
개시 신호
silent partner
익명 조합원
silver standard
은본위

SIMM (single in-line memory module) (computer)
단일 라인 메모리 모듈
simple interest
단리
simple trust
단순 신탁
simple yield
단순 이윤율
simulation
시뮬레이션, 모의 실험
single premium life insurance
일시불 보험료 생명보험
single-entry bookeeping
단식 부기
sinking fund
감채 기금
sit-down strike
연좌 파업, 농성 파업
site
현장
site audit
현장 감사
skill intensive
기술 집약적
skill obsolescence
기술의 노후화
slack
부진한, 불경기의
slander
중상, 명예 회손

sleeper
잠재적 우량주

sleeping beauty
잠재적 매입 대상 기업

slowdown
경제 성장의 둔화

slump
경기 침체

small business
소기업

small investor
소투자가

smoke clause
흡연 피해 조항

smokestack industry
굴뚝 산업

snowballing
(기업활동의) 갑작스런
확대

social insurance
사회보험

social responsibility
사회적 책임

socialism
사회주의

socially conscious investor
사회 인식형 투자가

soft currency
연화, 액체 통화

soft goods
비내구재, 섬유제품

soft market
약한 시장 현황

soft money
연화, 지폐

soft spot
약점

soil bank
토양은행

sole proprietorship
개인 상인, 개인 기업주

solvency
지불능력

source
원천, 자료, 원인

source evaluation
자료 평가

source worksheet *(computer)*
자료 워크시트

sources of funds
자금의 원천

sovereign risk
주권국 위험

space bar *(computer)*
스페이스 바

spamming *(computer)*
스펨 메일하기

span of control
관리 한계, 통제 한계

special agent
특별 대리인,
특별 심사관

special assignment
특별 임무,
특별 할당

special delivery
속달, 속달우편

special drawing rights
 (SDR)
특별 인출권

special handling
특별 취급

special purchase
특별 구입

special situation
특별한 상황

special warranty
 deed
특별 보증 인증서

specialist
전문가

specialty
 advertising
특제품 광고

specialty goods
전문품

specialty retailer
전문 소매점

specialty selling
특선품 판매

specialty shop
전문점

special-use
 permit
특별 사용 허가

specie
정금, 정화

specific identification
개별 원가 방법

specific performance
특별 이행, 구체적 이행

specific subsidy
특정 보조금

specification
사양(서), 명세서

speculative risk
투기적 위험

speech recognition
 (computer)
음성 인식

speedup
생산 증가

spell checker
 (computer)
철자법 검사 프로그램

spending money
용돈

spendthrift trust
낭비 방지 신탁

spider chart
 (computer)
스파이더 도표

spillover
과잉

spin-off
스핀오프

splintered authority
분열된 권위

split
주식 분할

split commission
분할 수수료

split shift
분할 근무

spokesperson
대변인

sponsor
스폰서, 출자자, 보증인

spot check
무작위 추출검사

spot commodity
현물 상품

spot delivery month
현물 양도의 달

spot market
현물 시장, 현물 거래 시장

spot price
처분 가격, 현지 가격

spot zoning
재용도 지정

spread
가격 폭

spread sheet
전개표, 운용표

spreading agreement
저당권 추가 설정 계약

squatter's rights
불법 점유자의 권리

squeeze
(경제적인) 압박, 긴축

stabilization
안정화

stacked column chart (computer)
연속막대 도표

staggered election
기차임기 선거

staggering maturities
만기 분산

stagnation
정체, 불경기

stake
이해 관계

stand-alone system
독립형 시스템

standard
표준, 기준

standard cost
표준 원가

standard deduction
표준 공제

standard deviation
표준 편차

standard industrial classification (SIC) system
표준 산업분류 제도

standard of living
생활 수준

standard time
표준 시간

standard wage rate
표준 임금율

standby *(computer)*
대기

standby fee
대기요금,

대체물 요금

standby loan
준비 융자

standing order
계속 주문

staple stock
주요 주식

start-up
개시,

신규 사업 개시

start-up screen
 (computer)
개시 화면

stated value
표시 가격

statement
명세서, 계산서

statement of affairs
업적 보고서, 자산부채표

statement of condition
대차대조표, 영업보고서

statement of partners'
 capital
동업자 자본계산서

static analysis
정적 분석, 정학 분석

static budget
고정 예산

static risk
고정적 위험

statistic
통계의, 통계치

statistical inference
통계적 추론

statistical sampling
통계적 표본조사

statistically significant
통계적으로 중요한

statistics
통계, 통계학, 통계 자료

status
지위, 자격, 정세

status bar
 (computer)
상태 바, 상태 표시줄

status symbol
지위의 상징, 권위의 상징

statute
제정법, 법령, 규칙

statute of frauds
사기 방지법

statute of limitations
소멸 시효, 소송 제기

기한법

statutory audit
법정 감사

statutory merger
법정 합병

statutory notice
법정 통지 기간

statutory voting	**stock market**
법정 투표	주식 시장
staying power	**stock option**
지구력, 내구력	스톡 옵션, 자사주 구입권
steady-growth method	**stock record**
균형 성장 방법	주식대장, 재고기록
steering	**stock symbol**
조종(하는 사람)	주식 기호
stepped-up basis	**stock turnover**
향상의 기준	상품 회전율
stipend, stipendiary	**stockbroker**
고정급, 봉급	주식 중매인
stipulation	**stockholder**
합의, 조항, 약정	주주
stochastic	**stockholder of record**
추계학의, 확율론적인	등록 주주
stock	**stockholder's derivative**
주식	**action**
stock certificate	주주 대표 소송
주권	**stockholder's equity**
stock dividend	주주 지분, 자기자본,
주식 배당	순자산
stock exchange	**stockout cost**
증권거래소	재고품절 손실
stock index future	**stockpile**
주가지수 선물	비축, 저장
stock insurance company	**stockpower**
주식보험회사	주식 양도 위임장
stock jobbing	**stockroom**
주식 중개	창고, 저장실
stock ledger	**stonewalling**
상품 원장	의사 방해, 협조 거부

stool pigeon
(경찰의) 정보원,
스파이
stop clause
(계약의)
정지조항
stop order
주식의 지정가 매매 주문,
정지 명령
stop payment
지불 정지
stop-loss reinsurance
초과 손해 재보험
store
상점, 비축
store brand
자가 브랜드 상품
straddle
동일 만기의 풋옵션과
콜옵션으로 동일 행사
가격에 동시에 매입하는
옵션
straight bill of lading
기명식 선하증권
straight time
정규 취업 시간
**straight-line method of
  depreciation**
정액법식 감가상각
straight-line production
직선법식 생산고

straphanger
(기차나 버스) 통근자
strategic planning
전략 계획
strategy
전략
**stratified random
  sampling**
계층화한 임의 추출
straw boss
감독 대행자, 실권없는
상사
straw man
위증자
street name
증권업자 명의로 된 증권
stretchout
노동 강화, 지연
strike
동맹 파업
strike benefits
파업 수당
strike notice
파업 통고
strike pay
파업 수당
strike price
행사 가격
strike vote
파업 투표
strikebreaker
파업 방해자

structural inflation
구조적 인플레이션
structure
구조, 조직
subcontractor
하청업자, 하청 계약자
subdirectory *(computer)*
서브디렉토리
subdivider
재분할자
subdividing
세분화
subdivision
재분할, 분할지
subject to mortgage
조건부 양도저당
sublease
전대
sublet
전대하다, 전대용 물건
subliminal advertising
잠재 의식에 의한 광고
submarginal
한계 이하의
suboptimize
차선의 상태로하다
subordinate debt
후순위 변제 채무
subordinated
후순위의
subordination
종속, 종속 관계, 후순위

subpoena
소환장, 소환하다
subrogation
대리, 대위변제
subroutine
서브루틴
subscript
 (computer)
서브스크립트
subscripted
 variable
배열, 하부의 변수
subscription
주식의 청약, 기부, 예약
구독
subscription price
응모 가격
subscription privilege
신주 인수 특권
subscription right
신주 인수권
subsequent event
후속 사건
subsidiary
보조의,
종속적인
subsidiary company
자회사, 종속회사
subsidiary ledger
보조원장
subsidy
보조금, 조성금

subsistence
생활, 생계비, 존재

substitution
대용품, 대체

substitution effect
대체 효과

substitution law
대체 법칙

substitution slope
교체 경사

subtenant
전대 차용인

subtotal
소계, 일부분의 합계

suggested retail price
제안 소매가격

suggestion system
제안 제도

suicide clause
자살 조항

suite *(computer)*
슈트

summons
소환장, 호출장

sunset industry
사양 산업

sunset provision
만기 조항

super now account
수퍼 나우 계좌, 일정 금액을
유지하면 높은 이자가
제공되는 구좌

super sinker bond
수퍼 싱커 본드, 단기
만기의 장기 쿠폰 채권

superintendent
관리자

supermarket
수퍼마켓

supersaver fare
특별 할인 요금

superscript *(computer)*
수퍼스크립트

superstore
대형 수퍼마켓

supplemental agreement
보조계약서

supplier
매입처, 공급자

supply
공급, 소모품

supply price
공급가액

supply-side economics
공급측 경제학

support level
저항선, 부양 수준

surcharge
추가 요금

surety bond
보증서

surge protector
 (computer)
서지 보호기

surplus
잉여금

surrender
권리의 포기

surrender, life insurance
생명보험의 해약

surtax
부가세

survey
조사하다, 측량하다

survey area
측량 지역

surveyor
감정인, 평가인

survivorship
생존자 재산권

suspended trading
보류 거래, 판매 정지

suspense account
미결산 계정

suspension
일시 정지, 정지

swap
스왑, 바꾸다, 교환

sweat equity
근로 제공, 근로 출자

sweatshop
노동착취공장

sweepstakes
스테이크 경마, 도박, 복권

sweetener
뇌물

swing shift
(3 교대제의) 오후 교대

switching
스위칭, 전환, 전환 매입

symbol bar *(computer)*
기호 바

sympathetic strike
동정 파업

syndicate
신디케이트,
기업 연합

syndication
신디케이트 조직

syndicator
인수 조합, 인수 은행단

synergy
시너지,
상승 작용

system
  (computer)
시스템

system administrator
  (computer)
시스템 관리자

systematic risk
체계적 위험

systematic sampling
체계적 표본조사

T

T statistic
t 통계량

tab key *(computer)*
탭키

table column
(computer)
테이블 칼럼

table field *(computer)*
테이블 필드

T-account
T 자형 계정

tactic
전법, 방책

tag sale
태그 세일

take
얻다, 획득하다, 채용하다

take a bath, take a
beating
크게 손해를 보다

take a flier
고공주를 사다

take a position
주식을 보유하다

take-home pay
각종 공제후 임금

takeoff
이륙

take-out loan, take-out
financing
건설 융자, 장기 부동산
담보 융자

takeover
기업 경영권 매수, 기업
취득

taking
취득, 소득

taking delivery
배달을 받음

taking inventory
재고조사

tally
할부, 계산

tangible asset
유형(고정) 자산

tangible personal property
유형 개인 재산

tank car
유조차

tape
테이프

target audience
청중

target file
목표 파일

target file *(computer)*
목표 파일

target group index
 (TGI)
목표 그룹 지수

target market
목표 시장

target price
목표 가격

tariff
관세, 세율,
요금

tariff war
관세 전쟁

task bar
작업 표시줄

task bar *(computer)*
작업 표시줄

task force
특별 작업반,
특별 위원회

task group
특별 과제 그룹

task list *(computer)*
태스크 리스트

task management
태스크 관리

task manager
 (computer)
태스크 매니저

tax
세금

tax abatement
감세

tax and loan account
조세 국채계정

tax anticipation bill (TAB)
조세 준비 증권, 조세 증권

tax anticipation note
 (TAN)
조세 준비 어음

tax base
과세 기준

tax bracket
과세 등급

tax credit
세액 공제, 세금 공제

tax deductible
과세 공제 항목

tax deduction
과세 공제

tax deed
공매 증서

tax deferred
과세 유예의,
납세 유예의

tax evasion
탈세

tax foreclosure
세금 유질처분

tax impact
조세 효과

tax incentive
조세 유인

tax incidence
조세 부담

tax lien
세금 담보권

tax loss carryback
(carryforward)
조세의 손금 소급
(이월)

tax map
과세 지도

tax planning
조세 계획,
절세 계획

tax preference
item
세금 우선 항목

tax rate
세율

tax return
세무 신고서, 납세 신고서

tax roll
과세 대장

tax sale
세금 체납 처분 공매

tax selling
세금 대책의 증권 매각

tax shelter
세금 피난 수단

tax stop
(임대인의) 납세 제한

tax straddle
세금 걸침

tax wedge
세금 쐐기

taxable income
과세소득

taxable year
과세 연도

taxation, interest on
dividends
배당 이자 과세

tax-exempt property
면세 재산

tax-exempt security
면세 증권

tax-free exchange
면세 교환

taxpayer
납세자

team building
팀 구축

team
management
팀 관리

teaser ad
유도 광고

teaser rate
미끼 금리,
유도 변동 금리

technical analysis
기술적 분석

technical rally
(증시의) 자발적 반발,
인위적 회복

technological
obsolescence
기술적 진부화

technological
unemployment
기술적 실업

technology
기술, 과학 기술

telecommunications
전자 통신

telemarketing
전화 판매

telephone switching
전화 교환

template
템플릿

tenancy
부동산권

tenancy at sufferance
인정한 부동산 임차권

tenancy at will
임의 부동산 임차권

tenancy by the
entirety
부부 전부 보유 부동산권

tenancy for years
정기 부동산권

tenancy in common
공유 부동산권

tenancy in severalty
단독 보유 부동산권

tenant
임차인

tenant finish-out
allowance
차용자 완료 할당금

tender
입찰, 제안

tender of delivery
인도의 배상금

tender offer
주식의 공개 매입

tenure
보유 기간,
보유 조건

tenure in land
토지 보유기간

term
기한, 기간, 조건

term certificate
정기예금증서

term life insurance
정기생명보험

term loan
기한 대부

term, amortization
채무 상환 기한

termination benefits
고용 종료 급부

terms
조건, 조항, 요금

test
검사, 시험

test market
시험 시장, 시험 판매

test statistic
시험통계

testament
유언, 유서

testamentary trust
유언 신탁

testate
유언, 유언된 유산

testator
남성 유언자

testcheck
시험 점검

testimonial
증명서, 추천장

testimonium
증명, 선언 증언

text editing *(computer)*
텍스트 편집

text processing *(computer)*
문서 처리

text wrap *(computer)*
텍스트 넘기기

thin market
한산한 시장

third market
(증권의) 제 3 시장

third party
제 3 자

third-party check
제 3 자 수표

third-party sale
제 3 자 판매

threshold-point ordering
한계점 주문

thrift institution
저축 금융기관

thrifty
절약

through rate
전 구간 운임

tick
(주식의) 가격 변동

ticker
시세 표시기

tie-in promotion
관련된 판매 촉진

tight market
핍박 마켓

tight money
금융 긴축

tight ship
질서와 통제가 이루어진 회사

till
돈상자

time card
작업 시간표

time deposit
정기예금, 저축성 예금

time draft
정기지급 어음

time is the essence
계약의 기한 엄수

time management	**title screen** *(computer)*
시간 관리	타이틀 스크린
time series analysis	**title search**
시계열 분석	부동산 소유권 조사
time series data	**title theory**
시계열 자료	소유권 이론
time value	**toggle key** *(computer)*
시간적 가치	토글 키
time-and-a-half	**tokenism**
50% 초과 근무 수당	명목주의, 형식주의
time-sharing	**toll**
시분할	사용료
timetable	**tomsbtone ad**
시간표, 계획표	묘비 광고
tip	**toner cartridge** *(computer)*
비밀 정보, 암시	토너 카트리지
title	**tool bar** *(computer)*
소유권, 권리의 원인	툴 바
title bar	**tool box** *(computer)*
제목 표시줄	툴 상자
title bar *(computer)*	**topping out**
타이틀 바	더 높을 수 없는 주가
title company	**tort**
부동산 소유권 보험회사	불법 행위, 개인 범죄
title defect	**total capitalization**
부동산 소유권 결함	총자본화, 총자산화
title insurance	**total loss**
부동산 소유권 보증	전 손실
title report	**total paid**
부동산 소유권 보고서	지불 총액
title screen	**total volume**
타이틀 스크린	총 거래고

touch screen *(computer)*
터치 스크린
trace, tracer
자취, 추적기
trackage
철도의 총선로, 궤도
사용료
trackball *(computer)*
트랙 볼
tract
지대, 영역, 주택 단지
trade
거래, 교환
trade acceptance
자기앞 환어음, 수출어음
인수
trade advertising
산업 광고, 유통 광고
trade agreement
무역 협약
trade barrier
무역 장애
trade credit
기업간 신용
trade date
약정일, 인수일
trade deficit (surplus)
무역 수지 적자 (흑자)
trade fixture
업무용 비품
trade magazine
업계지

trade rate
업자간 요금
trade secret
영업 비밀, 기업 비밀
trade show
상업 전시회
trade union
노동조합
trademark
상표
trade-off
거래, 교환, 흥정
trader
무역업자, 주식 매매인
trading authorization
거래 인가증
trading post
교역장, 무역소
trading range
거래 한도, 거래 범위
trading stamp
상품 인환 증지
trading unit
(주식의) 거래단위
traditional economy
전통 경제
tramp
부정기선
transaction
거래
transaction cost
거래 비용

transfer agent
증권 대리인

transfer development
  rights
개발권의 양도

transfer payment
이전 지출, 양도 지불

transfer price
양도 가격, 이전 가격

transfer tax
자산 이전세,
자산 거래세

translate
번역

transmit a virus
바이러스를 전염시키다

transmit a virus
  (computer)
바이러스를
전송하다

transmittal letter
송장

transnational
초국가권

transportation
운송

treason
반역(죄)

treasurer
재무부장, 경리부장

tree diagram
수형도

trend
동향, 경향

trend chart
(computer)
경향 차트

trend line
추세선

trespass
불법 침해

trial and error
시행 오차

trial balance
시산표

trial offer
시제품 제공

trial subscriber
시험 구매자

trigger point
트리거 점, 덤핑조사의
계기점

trigger price
트리거 가격, 지표 가격

triple-net lease
임차인이 모든 경비를
부담하는 리스

Trojan horse (computer)
트로이 목마

troubled debt
restructuring
불량 채무의 재조정

troubleshooter
조정자, 중재자, 수리계

troubleshooting
 (computer)
문제 처리, 수리
trough
경기주기의 저점
true lease
진정한 리스
true to
 scale
확장 또는 축소할 수 있는
true to scale
 (computer)
확장 또는 축소할 수 있는
truncation
끝을 잘라냄, 끊음
trust
신탁
trust account
신탁 계정,
신탁 재산
trust certificate
신탁 수익증권
trust company
신탁회사
trust deed
신탁증서
trust fund
신탁기금
trust, discretionary
재량신탁
trust, general
 management
일반관리 투자신탁

trustee
피신탁자, 신탁의 수탁자,
관재인, 이사
trustee in bankruptcy
파산 관재인
trustor
신탁 설정자
truth in lending act
대부조항 표시법
turkey
실패한 투자, 실패작
turn off *(computer)*
끄기, 끄다
turn on *(computer)*
켜기, 켜다
turnaround
턴어라운드, 전환
turnaround time
턴어라운드 기간, 전환
기간
turnkey
턴키 방식의, 완전인수
방식의
turnover
매출액, 회전율,
수확량
twisting
생명보험의 부당 계약
two percent rule
2 % 법칙
two-tailed test
양측 검정

tycoon
타이쿤, 대군
typeface *(computer)*
활자체

type-over mode
 (computer)
덮어쓰기 모드

U

umbrella liability
 insurance
포괄적 책임보험

unappropriated retained
 earnings
미처리 보유 소득

unbalanced growth
불균형 성장

unbiased estimator
공평한 추정량

uncollected funds
미결제자금

uncollectible
회수 불능

unconsolidated
 subsidiary
비연결 자회사

under the counter
암거래되는,

비밀의

underapplied
 overhead
과소 부가 간접비

undercapitalization
과소 출자

underclass
사회의 저변,

하층 계급

underemployed
불완전 취업의

underground economy
지하 경제

underinsured
불충분한 보험 가입

underline
 (computer)
밑줄, 하선

underlying debt
우선 채무, 제일 채무

underlying mortgage
우선 저당, 제일 저당

underlying security
기초 유가증권

underpay
임금을 충분히 주지 않다

undervalued
과소 평가된

underwriter
증권 인수회사

underwriting spread
인수 수수료

undiscounted
비할인, 정상

undivided interest
비분할 지분

undivided profit
비분할 이익
undue influence
부당한 영향력, 부당한
위압
unearned discount
선수 공제 이자
**unearned income
(revenue)**
선수 이익(소득)
unearned increment
(재산의) 자연증가
unearned interest
선수 이자
**unearned
premium**
선수 보험료
unemployable
고용할 수 없는
**unemployed labor
force**
실업 근로자
unemployment
실업
**unencumbered
property**
저당이나 부채가 없는
부동산
unexpired cost
미소비 원가
unfair competition
불공정 경쟁

**unfavorable balance of
trade**
무역수지의 적자, 수입
초과
unfreeze
(자금이나 예산의) 동결을
해제하다
unified estate and gift tax
통합된 유산 증여세
unilateral contract
일방적 계약
unimproved property
미개발 부동산
**unincorporated
association**
비법인 단체
unique impairment
특이한 장애,
특이한 손상
unissued stock
미발행 주식
unit
구성 단위
unit of trading
판매 단위
unitary elasticity
단일 탄력성
unit-labor cost
단위 노동 비용
**units-of-production
method**
생산고 비례법

unity of command
명령의 통일성

universal life insurance
유니버설 생명보험

universal product code (UPC)
통일 상품 코드

unlisted security
비상장 증권

unloading
처분

unoccupancy
비거주, 비점유

unpaid dividend
미지불 배당금

unrealized profit (loss)
인식되지 않은 이익 (손실)

unrecorded deed
미등록 증서

unrecoverable *(computer)*
복구 불능

unrecovered cost
회수 불능 원가

unsecured debt
무담보 채무

unwind a trade
역거래

up front
선불의, 선행 투자의

up tick
상승 기운

update *(computer)*
갱신

upgrade *(computer)*
업그레이드

upgrade software *(computer)*
업그레이드 소프트웨어

upgrading
개량

upkeep
유지, 부양

upload *(computer)*
업로드

upper case letter *(computer)*
대문자

upright format *(computer)*
직립형 포멧

upside potential
상승 가능성

upswing
상승 기세

uptrend
상승 경향, 상향

upwardly mobile
향상 지향의

urban
도시의

urban renewal
도시 재개발

useful life
내용 연수

user *(computer)*
사용자, 이용자

user authorization
(computer)
사용자 허가

user manual *(computer)*
사용자 안내서

usufructuary right
사용권

usury
고리 대금, 폭리

utility
유익, 효용, 공익 사업,
공공 시설

utility easement
공공 시설 지역권

utility program *(computer)*
유틸리티 프로그램

V

vacancy rate
공실율
vacant
빈
vacant land
공한지
vacate
비우다, 무효화하다
valid
유효, 유효한
valuable
consideration
유가약인, 대가
valuable papers (records)
 insurance
유가증권 보험
valuation
감정 평가, 사정, 평가액
value date
어음 결제일
value in exchange
교환 가치
value line investment
 survey
가치라인의 투자 조사
value-added tax
부가가치세
variable
변수

variable annuity
변동 연금
variable cost
변동 원가, 가변적 비용
variable interest rate
변동 금리
variable life insurance
변액 생명보험
variable pricing
변동 가격 설정
variable-rate mortgage
 (VRM)
변동 금리형 저당
variables sampling
변동 견본 추출
variance
차이, 분산
variety store
잡화점
velocity
속도
vendee
매수인,
인수인
vendor
매각인, 행상인
vendor's lien
매각인 선취 특권

venture
모험, 투기, 모험적 사업,
투기적 사업

venture capital
벤처 캐피탈

venture team
신규 사업 팀

verbations
동사화

vertical analysis
수직 분석

vertical discount
수직 할인

**vertical management
  structure**
수직 경영구조

vertical promotion
수직 승진

**vertical
  specialization**
수직적 분업

vertical union
산업별 노동조합

vested interest
확정적 권리,
기득권익

vesting
수령권

vicarious liability
대리 책임, 사용자 책임

vice-president
부사장, 부총재

video conference
  (computer)
화상 회의, 영상 회의

video graphics board
  (computer)
비디오 그래픽 보드

violation
위반, 침해

virtual memory
  (computer)
가상 기억장치

visual interface *(computer)*
영상 화면 인터페이스

vocational guidance
직업 지도, 취업 지도

voice mail *(computer)*
음성 우편,
보이스 메일

voice recognition
  (computer)
음성 인식

voidable
취소 가능한

volatile
극심한 가격 변동

volume
생산량, 제조량, 용량,
볼륨

volume discount
수량 할인

**volume merchandise
  allowance**
대량 구입 할인

voluntary accumulation
 plan
자발적 누적 계획
voluntary bankruptcy
자발적 파산,
자발적 해산
voluntary conveyance
임의 양도, 무상 양도
voluntary lien
자발적 선취 특권

voting right
의결권
voting stock
의결권이 있는 주식
voting trust certificate
의결권이 있는 신탁증서
voucher
거래 증빙서
voucher register
지불전표 기입장

W

wage
임금, 급료

wage assignment
급료 공제

wage bracket
급료 범위

wage ceiling
최고 임금

wage control
임금 통제

wage floor
최저 임금

wage freeze
임금 동결

wage incentive
장려급, 능률급

wage rate
임금율

wage scale
임금 일람표

wage stabilization
임금 안정화

wage-push
 inflation
임금상승에 의한
인플레이션

waiver
권리 포기

walkout
동맹 파업, 항의 퇴장

wallflower
비인기 주식

wallpaper *(computer)*
배경화면

ware
상품, 제품

warehouse
창고, 상품 보관소,
대형상점

warm boot/start
 (computer)
웜 부트

warranty
워런티, 주식 매수권, 신주
인수권

warranty deed
증서상의 담보책임,
보증증서

warranty of habitability
거주성 보증

warranty of
 merchantability
상품성의 보증

wash sale
절세 거래, 워시 세일,
증권의 가장 매매

waste
작업 폐물
wasting asset
소모성 자산, 감모자산
watch list
감시 사항 일람표,
watered stock
혼수 주식, 가공 자본
waybill
화물 인환증, 화물의 송장
weak market
약세 시장 현황, 하향 시장
weakest link theory
최약 연결설
wear and tear
마모
wearout factor
마모 요소
web browser *(computer)*
웹 브라우저
web server *(computer)*
웹 서버
welfare state
복지국가
when issued
발행일 거래
whipsawed
이중으로 손해를 본
white goods
대형 가정용품
white knight
백마의 기사

white paper
백서, 공식 보고서
whole life insurance
종신 생명보험
whole loan
전부의 대부
wholesaler
도매업자, 대리점
widget
이런 저런 제품, 소형장치
widow-and-orphan stock
안정 배당주
wildcat drilling
투기적 시추
wildcat strike
무모한 파업
will
유언서, 의도
windfall profit
불로소득,
우발이익
winding up
해산, 청산
window *(computer)*
윈도우즈
window dressing
분식 회계
windows application
 (computer)
윈도우즈 응용
wipeout
대패, 참패

wire house
와이어 하우스, 통신
시스템이 설치된
증권회사 지점
withdrawal
인출
withdrawal plan
인출 계획
withholding
원천징수
withholding tax
원천 징수세, 원천 과세
without recourse
소유권이 없는
wizard *(computer)*
마법사
word processing
(computer)
문서 처리
word wrapping *(computer)*
단어 넘기기
work force
전 종업원, 전 노동 인구
work in progress
재공품
work order
제조 지시서, 작업 지시서
work permit
취업 허가, 근로 허가
work
simplification
업무 간소화, 작업 간소화

work station
워크 스테이션
work stoppage
작업 정지
work week
주 노동 시간
working capital
운전 자본
workload
작업 부하
workout
워크아웃, 기업의 구조 조정
worksheet
정산표
worksheet
(computer)
워크시트
world bank
세계은행
world wide web (www)
(computer)
월드 와이드 웹
worm
(computer)
웜 바이러스
worth
가치
wraparound
mortgage
포괄적 저당권
wraparound type
(computer)
넘기기 유형

writ
영장

writ of error
오심 영장

write error
  (computer)
쓰기 오류

write-protected
  (computer)
쓰기 방지된

writer
옵션 판매자, 보험업자

write-up
자산 가치의 증가

writing naked
주식을 소유하지 않는
옵션 판매

written-down value
감가상각후 가격

XYZ

x-coordinate
 (computer)
X 좌표

y-coordinate
 (computer)
Y 좌표

year-end
연말

year-end dividend
연도말 배당

year-to-date (YTD)
연간, 연중

yellow dog contract
황견계약, 노조에
가입하지 않겠다는
조건하의 고용계약

yellow goods
(이익률이 높은) 내구성
소비재

yellow sheets
장외 거래 회사채의
거래기록

yield
수율, 이율, 산출, 수확

yield curve
수익률 곡선

yield equivalence
수익률 등가

yield spread
수익률 격차

yield to average life
(채권의) 평균 수명 수익률

yield to call
상환 이익률

yield-to-mature (YTM)
만기 이율

yo-yo stock
가격이 급변하는 주식

z score
표준득점

zero coupon bond
제로 쿠폰채, 무이자
할인채

zero economic growth
경제의 제로 성장

zero lot line
건물이 경계선에 선
부지의 경계선

zero population growth
 (ZPG)
인구의 제로 성장

zero-base budgeting
 (ZBB)
제로 베이스 예산

zero-sum game
제로섬 게임

zone of employment
고용 지역

zoning
토지 용도 지정, 건축 규제

Order Form

Fax orders (Send this form): (301) 424-2518. Telephone orders: Call 1 (800) 822-3213
[in Maryland: (301) 424-7737]
E-mail orders: spbooks@aol.com or books@schreiberpublishing.com
Mail orders to: Schreiber Publishing, 51 Monroe St., Suite 101, Rockville MD 20850
USA

Please send the following books, programs, and/or a free catalog. I understand that I may
return any of them for a full refund, for any reason, no questions asked:

❑ **The Translator's Handbook** 5th Revised Edition - $25.95

❑ **Spanish Business Dictionary** - Multicultural Spanish - $24.95

❑ **German Business Dictionary** - $24.95

❑ **French (France and Canada) Business Dictionary** - $24.95

❑ **Chinese Business Dictionary** - $24.95

❑ **Arabic Business Dictionary** - $24.95

❑ **Italian Business Dictionary** - $24.95

❑ **Korean Business Dictionary** - $24.95

❑ **Japanese Business Dictionary** - $24.95

❑ **Russian Business Dictionary** - $24.95

❑ **Global Business Dictionary (English, French, German, Russian, Japanese, Chinese)** - $33.95

❑ **Spanish Chemical and Pharmaceutical Glossary** - $29.95

❑ **The Translator's Self-Training Program** (circle the language/s of your choice): Spanish   French   German   Japanese   Chinese   Italian   Portuguese   Russian   Arabic   Hebrew - $69.00

❑ **The Translator's Self-Training Program Spanish Medical** - $69.00

❑ **The Translator's Self-Training Program Spanish Legal** - $69.00

❑ **The Translator's Self-Training Program - German Patents** - $69.00

❑ **The Translator's Self-Training Program - Japanese Patents** - $69.00

❑ **Multicultural Spanish Dictionary** - How Spanish Differs from Country to Country - $24.95

❑ **21st Century American English Compendium** - The "Odds and Ends" of American English Usage - $24.95

❑ **Dictionary of Medicine French/English** - Over one million terms in medical terminology - $179.50

Name: _____

Address: _____

City: _____ State: _____ Zip: _____

Telephone: _____ e-mail: _____

Sales tax: Please add 5% sales tax in Maryland

U.S. Shipping (est.): $4.50 for the first book and $2 for each additional book

Payment: ❑ Check ❑ Credit card: ❑ Visa ❑ MasterCard

Card number: _____

Name on card: _____ Exp. Date: ___ / ___